A Worshiper's Journey

A Worshiper's Journey

Pursuing God's Heart Through a Life of Worship

Tim McGuire

RESOURCE *Publications* · Eugene, Oregon

A WORSHIPER'S JOURNEY
Pursuing God's Heart Through a Life of Worship

Resource Publications
An Imprint of Wipf and Stock Publishers
199 W. 8th Ave., Suite 3
Eugene, OR 97401

www.wipfandstock.com

PAPERBACK ISBN: 979-8-3852-5277-0
HARDCOVER ISBN: 979-8-3852-5278-7
EBOOK ISBN: 979-8-3852-5279-4

VERSION NUMBER 07/08/25

To the memory of my father-in-law, Larry,
and mother-in-law, Linda,
and to my brother-in-law, Max, and sisters-in-law,
Penny, Vicky, and Judy—
thank you for filling my life with
the wonder and joy of music.
Your voices and hearts helped shape
my own worship journey.

And to the memory of my stepdad, Doyle—
you taught me that worship is more than a melody sung;
it's a life poured out in service to others.
Your quiet strength and selfless love were hymns of their own.

This book is for you—with deepest gratitude and love.

Contents

Preface: A Life of Worship in All Things

EVERY MORNING, AS OUR two youngest sons step out of the house, my wife speaks a phrase that has become a cherished tradition: *"Praise the Lord in all you say and do."* It's a simple sentence, yet its power lies in its profound truth. These words encapsulate the heart of Colossians 3:17, which urges us, *"And whatever you do, whether in word or deed, do it all in the name of the Lord Jesus, giving thanks to God the Father through him."*

At first glance, these words may seem like an ideal to strive for, but when we pause to consider their weight, we see they are a call to a radically different way of life. They challenge us to live with intentionality, viewing every action and every word as an opportunity to glorify God. But how often do we actually live this way? How often do we confine the act of praise and worship to Sunday mornings or a quick prayer before meals?

For many years, my own understanding of worship was limited. Growing up, I believed worship was something you did at church—a time set aside for singing hymns, listening to sermons, and taking communion. It was easy to compartmentalize worship, placing it in a neat little box labeled *Sunday Morning Service,* while the rest of the week became "real life." Worship, I thought, belonged in the sacred space of the church building, while the ordinary moments of life—the errands, the deadlines, the challenges—were entirely separate.

But as I grew in my faith and encountered the realities of life, I began to see how narrow and incomplete this view was. Worship is not an event; it's a way of being. It's not confined to a specific time or place but is meant to permeate every aspect of our lives. Worship happens not just in the melodies of a hymn but in the silence of a heartfelt prayer. It happens in the way we treat others, in the integrity of our actions, and in the gratitude we express even in difficult circumstances. This understanding transformed my perspective and deepened my walk with Christ.

Why I Wrote This Book

The idea for this book began to take shape during one of the most challenging seasons of my life. As a Navy Chief, I spent over two decades in environments that tested my faith, endurance, and resilience. I witnessed firsthand the struggles of maintaining spiritual integrity in a world that often felt anything but sacred. Yet, even in the midst of those challenges, I saw glimpses of God's presence—moments when worship was not only possible but necessary.

One such moment stands out vividly. During a particularly intense deployment, I found myself leading a small group of sailors in a makeshift worship service. We were far from home, surrounded by uncertainty, and burdened by the weight of our responsibilities. Yet, in that moment, as we lifted our voices in praise, I realized that worship was not about the setting or the circumstances. It was about our hearts aligning with God's truth, finding hope and purpose in His presence.

This realization became a cornerstone of my faith and a driving force behind this book. I want to share what I've learned about worship—not as an expert, but as someone who has wrestled with its meaning and experienced its transformative power. My hope is that this book will inspire you to see your own life as a canvas for worship, where every moment becomes an opportunity to glorify God.

What You Will Gain?

This book is not just about theology; it's about practice. It's about taking the timeless truths of Scripture and applying them to the realities of everyday life. Through personal stories, biblical insights, and practical applications, I aim to show how worship can become a lifestyle—one that brings purpose, joy, and alignment with God's will.

Here's what you can expect to gain from this book:

1. **A Renewed Perspective on Worship:** You'll discover that worship is not limited to singing or attending church but is woven into every aspect of your life. Whether you're at work, at home, or in a season of struggle, you can honor God through your actions, words, and attitudes.

2. **Biblical Foundations:** Each chapter is rooted in Scripture, offering a deeper understanding of what it means to worship "in spirit and in truth" (John 4:23). You'll explore passages that challenge and encourage you to live a life of continual praise.

3. **Practical Tools for Growth:** The study guide provided with this book is designed to help you engage with the material on a deeper level. With reflection questions, action steps, and prompts for journaling, it's a resource for personal or group study that will help you apply what you've learned.

4. **Encouragement for the Journey:** Worship is not always easy, especially in the face of hardship. This book offers encouragement for those times when praising God feels like the last thing you want to do. Through stories of faith and perseverance, you'll be reminded that God is worthy of praise in every season.

The Journey Ahead

As you begin this journey, I encourage you to approach it with an open heart. Allow God to speak to you through these pages, challenging and transforming the way you see worship. Whether you are a seasoned believer or just beginning to explore what it means to follow Christ, there is something here for you.

We will explore questions like:

- What does it mean to worship God in the mundane moments of life?

- How can our actions, decisions, and attitudes reflect a heart of worship?

- What role does gratitude play in a life of praise?

- How can we honor God in seasons of difficulty or doubt?

Each chapter builds upon the last, leading you deeper into an understanding of worship as a lifestyle. Along the way, you'll find opportunities to reflect, journal, and pray, allowing the truths of Scripture to take root in your heart.

A Personal Invitation

This book is not just a collection of ideas; it's a conversation. It's an invitation to walk with me as we learn what it means to praise the Lord in all we say and do. It's an opportunity to discover the joy and freedom that come from living a life that honors Him.

As you read these pages and engage with the study guide, I pray that you will experience a renewed sense of purpose and a deeper connection with God. May this journey lead you to a life of worship that transcends circumstances, bringing glory to Him in every moment.

Let's take this journey together, learning to live as true worshipers, created to glorify God in all things. Whether you are navigating the busyness of daily life, enduring a season of difficulty, or celebrating a time of abundance, my prayer is that this book will inspire and equip you to live a life that honors Him.

So let us begin, with hearts full of gratitude and minds ready to be transformed, as we step into the joy and beauty of a life lived in worship. Together, let us discover what it means to truly praise the Lord in all we say and do.

Chapter 1: The Essence of Worship

"Yet a time is coming and has now come when the true worshipers will worship the Father in the Spirit and in truth, for they are the kind of worshipers the Father seeks."

—JOHN 4:23

I WAS AROUND TWELVE years old when I first led worship at the small church my mother attended. Even now, I remember the rush of nerves and excitement as I stepped onto the stage, standing behind the pulpit, as the congregation waited for the first note. Our services were predictable—beginning with a hymn, then a prayer, followed by another song, leading into communion. This well-rehearsed routine was, to my young mind, the essence of worship. I thought I understood what it meant: a carefully orchestrated series of actions we performed each Sunday.

Years later, I began to realize how limited my understanding had been. Worship, I had thought, was confined to those sacred few hours in a church building. It was something we did—an action, a part of the service. But as I matured and experienced the joys and trials of life, I began to grasp a deeper, richer understanding of worship. It wasn't merely a ritual or an event. Worship, I came to see, was a journey—one that involved not only my outward actions but my inner being, my very soul. This chapter marks the beginning of exploring what worship truly means: the discovery of God's presence in our lives and the reflection of our heart's posture toward Him.

The Heart of Worship

At the core of worship is something far more profound than singing songs or reciting prayers. It is about connecting with God in the most authentic and intimate way. Over the next few chapters, we will explore this journey together, examining how we, as believers, can ensure that our worship honors God and reflects a deep, heartfelt connection with Him. We will dig into the essence of worship: what it means to worship in spirit and in truth, and how we can align our lives to reflect that truth.

John 4:23 is the cornerstone of this understanding: "Yet a time is coming and has now come when the true worshipers will worship the Father in the Spirit and in truth, for they are the kind of worshipers the Father seeks." Jesus spoke these words during His conversation with the Samaritan woman at the well. In this profound moment, He reveals that worship is not about a specific location, a ritual, or outward performance. It is not bound by geography or cultural norms. True worship is about the heart—approaching God with sincerity, humility, and authenticity.

In Hebrew, the concept of worship is not encapsulated by a single word. Instead, the language offers multiple words for worship, each expressing a different nuance or action. Some refer to bowing down in reverence, others to serving with a willing heart, while still others focus on adoration and awe. This diversity reflects the multifaceted nature of worship itself—it is not confined to a single expression but is instead a dynamic and ongoing dialogue between us and God.

Worship in Spirit

To worship "in spirit" means that worship transcends physical rituals and places. It is not limited by what we can see or touch.

Instead, it is a deep, internal connection between our spirit and God's Spirit. True worship flows from within, from a heart genuinely seeking to honor and glorify God. It is a deeply personal and intimate act, one that is not based on the external but rooted in the internal state of our souls.

Earlier I admitted how limited my understanding of worship was. I believed it was something we did in a specific place and in a particular way—singing hymns, praying, and participating in communion. But as I grew older, I began to see that true worship is not confined to those acts. Worship can take place anywhere, at any time. It is the expression of a heart that is in communion with God, whether through song, prayer, or simply living a life that reflects His love and truth.

In the context of "spirit," worship becomes more than just an action—it becomes an attitude, a way of living. Every moment of our lives can be an act of worship if our hearts are tuned to God. Whether we are at work, at home, or walking through nature, we can worship God by acknowledging His presence, seeking His guidance, and offering our praise.

Worship in Truth

Worship "in truth" means that our worship must be grounded in the reality of who God is. It cannot be based solely on emotion, preference, or tradition. While emotions can play a role in worship, they should never be the foundation of it. Instead, worship in truth is a response to the reality of God's character as revealed in Scripture. It is a recognition of His holiness, His love, His grace, and His power.

Truth in worship requires that we approach God with an accurate understanding of who He is. This means that we cannot reduce worship to our own ideas of what feels good or right. Instead, we must align our worship with the truth of God's Word. Worship that is rooted in truth is anchored in an unwavering commitment to God's revealed character and His plan for redemption through Jesus Christ.

This understanding calls us to worship with both our minds and hearts engaged. Worship is not merely an emotional experience but also an intellectual one. We are called to know God—His attributes, His promises, His works—and to let that knowledge inform and fuel our worship.

What Worship Is Not

It is easy to misunderstand worship if we focus only on its outward expressions. For many, worship has been reduced to the music played during church services. While music is undoubtedly a powerful vehicle for worship, it is not the entirety of it. Worship is not just music, nor is it something that happens only during a church service. It is not confined to a specific ritual, routine, or location.

One of the most common misconceptions about worship is that it is something we do only in church. While corporate worship is essential and commanded in Scripture, worship itself is not limited to a physical building. True worship can happen anywhere—at home, at work, in the car, or even out in nature. Worship is not about where we are; it is about the condition of our hearts before God.

Worship is also not about performance. You do not need to be a talented musician or a skilled singer to worship God. The most beautiful worship in God's eyes is not the most polished performance but the most sincere offering of a heart wholly devoted to Him. Worship is not about what we do, but why we do it. It is about the heart behind the action, not the action itself.

Worship as a Relationship

Worship ongoing relationship, a continual dialogue between us and God. Worship is our response to God's love, His grace, and His presence in our lives. It is an expression of gratitude, adoration, and reverence for who He is and what He has done.

This ongoing dialogue is not limited to words or songs. Worship is expressed in how we live our lives, how we treat others, and how we steward the gifts and resources God has given us. Every act of obedience, every choice to love and serve others, every moment of surrender to God's will is an act of worship. Worship is, at its core, a lifestyle—one that is lived in constant communion with God.

Think of the relationships that matter most to you—whether with a spouse, a parent, a child, or a close friend. These relationships are built on trust, communication, and time spent together. The same is true in our relationship with God. Worship is the time we spend with Him, the trust we place in Him, and the expression of our hearts toward Him. It is not confined to a single activity or time of day but is the ongoing overflow of our love and gratitude for Him.

The Journey of Worship

Worship is a journey—one that we are all on as believers. It is not a one-time event or a weekly occurrence. It is a lifelong process of drawing closer to God, learning more about His character, and responding to Him with love and adoration. Along this journey, there will be moments of joy and celebration, as well as times of sorrow and struggle. But in every season, worship remains the constant thread that connects us to God.

Worship in the midst of pain and hardship is perhaps the most powerful form of worship. It declares that God is worthy of our praise, even when our circumstances are far from ideal. Worship during times of trial is an act of faith, a statement that we trust in God's goodness and sovereignty, even when we cannot see the outcome.

The journey of worship requires surrender. It calls us to lay down our pride, our preferences, and our agendas. It demands that we focus on God, even when distractions abound. But this journey is worth every step because it leads us into a deeper, more intimate relationship with the One who created us, loves us, and calls us His own.

Worship is not about a particular style or a specific place. It is not something that can be reduced to an event or a ritual. True worship is a reflection of our relationship with God—a relationship built on love, trust, and authenticity.

Chapter 2: A Lifestyle of Worship

"Therefore, I urge you, brothers and sisters, in view of God's mercy, to offer your bodies as a living sacrifice, holy and pleasing to God—this is your true and proper worship."

—ROMANS 12:1

ONE OF THE MOST foundational elements of worship begins with the individual. The worship of God is not limited to songs or rituals but extends to the transformation of one's entire life—starting with personal holiness. Worship becomes not a momentary act, but a lifestyle, an ongoing dedication of oneself to God. The Apostle Paul emphasizes this in Romans the twelfth chapter, "Therefore, I urge you, brothers and sisters, in view of God's mercy, to offer your bodies as a living sacrifice, holy and pleasing to God—this is your true and proper worship." In this passage, Paul highlights that true worship is not merely an outward expression but an inward offering of one's entire being.

But what does it mean to offer ourselves as a "living sacrifice"? How do we, as followers of Christ, incorporate this kind of worship into our daily lives? Paul's next verse offers insight into how we can please God. In Romans 12:2, he continues, "Do not conform to the pattern of this world, but be transformed by the renewing of your mind. Then you will be able to test and approve what God's will is—his good, pleasing and perfect will."

This idea of a renewed mind is the basis of how we live a life of worship. It demands a total transformation, and from this transformation flow three essential aspects of worship: our actions, our attitudes, and our decisions. Each of these is a reflection of our devotion and reverence to God.

Worship in Our Actions

The saying "actions speak louder than words" holds particular weight when we talk about living a life that is pleasing to God. If worship is truly a lifestyle, our actions must reflect that. How we live out our faith is just as important as the songs we sing or the prayers we offer. Our actions often serve as the first testimony to others of our faith. People watch the way we live, particularly those who know we profess to be Christians. Our actions, whether positive or negative, speak volumes about the depth of our faith and our commitment to God.

During my time in the Navy, this was a challenging area for me. There were moments when I felt like I was living two separate lives. On the one hand, I was "the" Christian at church, participating in worship and trying to live out my faith. On the other hand, I was the sailor at work, deeply immersed in the culture and lifestyle of military life—a "sailor's sailor," as the phrase goes. It felt as though my faith was compartmentalized, with one version of me at church and another version at work. My actions at work did not reflect the worship and faith I professed on Sundays.

This disconnection between my faith and my actions highlighted a key aspect of worship: worship isn't confined to the church pew. It must permeate every aspect of our daily lives, including how we act in the workplace, with our families, and even in moments of solitude. Our actions must reflect a heart that is fully surrendered to God. True worship means that our faith is evident in everything we do.

In Romans 12:3-8, Paul addresses the importance of humble service, emphasizing that we are all part of one body, with different gifts and functions. Humility in service is an act of worship. We are called to serve one another not for personal gain, but for the glory of God. Similarly, Romans 12:9-21 speaks of acts of love—another form of worship in action. Love, in its truest form, is sacrificial, and when we love others in this way, we mirror Christ's love for us. Lastly, Romans 13:1-7 touches on submission, reminding us that submitting to authority, when done in reverence to God, is an act of worship. Each of these actions—humble service, sacrificial love, and submission—are ways we worship God through our daily lives.

Worship in Our Attitudes

While actions are critical, worship is incomplete if it does not begin with the heart. Attitude is the unseen foundation upon which our actions are built. A person can go through the motions of worship, performing acts of service, love, and submission, but if the heart is not aligned with God, those actions become hollow. Worship starts from within; it is an attitude of reverence, humility, and surrender to God's will.

In Isaiah 29:13, God warns against a kind of worship that is purely external: "These people come near to me with their mouth and honor me with their lips, but their hearts are far from me. Their worship of me is based on merely human rules they have been taught." This verse speaks to the danger of worship becoming a performance, an outward show without the inward transformation. It is possible to go through the motions of worship—singing the songs, saying the right words—while our hearts remain distant from God.

True worship begins with the attitude of our hearts—something I constantly have to work on. It's an attitude rooted in reverence, recognizing God's holiness and absolute authority. It seeks to honor Him not just through outward actions but through the deepest thoughts and desires within. A worshipful heart is marked by humility, acknowledging our complete dependence on God. It remains open to His correction and leadership, willing to surrender—even when obedience is hard.

9

During my military service, I often found myself struggling with my attitude toward certain aspects of life. In the high-stress environment of deployment, it was easy to become cynical, bitter, or self-reliant. These attitudes created barriers between me and God, even when I was outwardly going through the motions of being a Christian. It was in those moments that I had to examine my heart and ask, "Am I truly worshiping God in my attitude? Or am I merely putting on a façade?"

The answer is clear: God desires worshipers whose hearts are fully committed to Him. Worshiping God in our attitude means that we approach every situation with a heart of humility, gratitude, and dependence on God. It means that we are quick to repent when we stray and quick to forgive when others wrong us. It means that we keep our hearts tender and open to the Spirit's leading, always seeking to glorify God in everything we do.

Worship in Our Decisions

At first glance, decisions may not seem directly connected to worship. However, if we consider that worship is the offering of our entire being to God, then the choices we make—the decisions that shape our lives—are a crucial part of how we worship. Every decision, whether big or small, reflects what we value, what we prioritize, and ultimately, whom we worship.

In the life of a Christian, decision-making should be characterized by a deep dependency on God. This dependency begins with seeking God's will in prayer and discernment. We are called to submit our plans, desires, and decisions to God, trusting that His will is perfect. As worshipers, our decisions must flow out of a heart that is fully surrendered to God's control.

I realize that many of the decisions I made were based on self-reliance rather than dependence on God. In moments of stress or uncertainty, it was easy to fall back on my own understanding, making decisions based on what seemed right in the moment. However, this self-reliance often led to regret or missteps. The moments when

I chose to seek God's guidance in prayer, submitting my will to His, were the moments that led to peace and clarity.

Worship in our decision-making starts with prayer. Before making any significant choice, we must come before God, seeking His will and asking for discernment. Proverbs 3:5-6 reminds us to "trust in the Lord with all your heart and lean not on your own understanding; in all your ways submit to him, and he will make your paths straight." This passage underscores the importance of submitting our decisions to God, trusting that He knows what is best for us.

Moreover, worship in decision-making also involves aligning our choices with God's Word. The Bible is full of wisdom and guidance, offering principles for how we should live our lives. Whether it's decisions related to our career, relationships, or personal conduct, God's Word provides a framework for making choices that honor Him. A heart of worship is one that seeks to obey God's Word, even when it's difficult or countercultural.

In my own journey, I have learned that worship in decision-making is not always about making the "right" choice but about making the choice that honors God. Sometimes, this means choosing the path of humility over pride, the path of service over self-interest, or the path of obedience over convenience. Each of these decisions, when made with a heart of worship, brings us closer to God and reflects our desire to live lives that are pleasing to Him.

The worship journey begins with the individual, and it encompasses far more than what happens during a church service. It is a transformation of the whole self—our actions, our attitudes, and our decisions. As Paul writes in Romans 12:1-2, worship is about offering ourselves as living sacrifices, not conforming to the world, but being transformed by the renewing of our minds.

Our actions reflect our worship when they are marked by humble service, sacrificial love, and submission. Our attitudes reflect our worship when they are characterized by humility, gratitude, and dependence on God. Our decisions reflect our worship when they are made in prayerful submission to God's will, guided by His Word.

As we continue on this worship journey, may our actions, attitudes, and decisions be a living testimony of our devotion to God, bringing Him glory in every aspect of our lives.

Chapter 3: **Worship Is a Weapon**

"After consulting the people, Jehoshaphat appointed men to sing to the Lord and to praise him for the splendor of his holiness as they went out at the head of the army, saying: 'Give thanks to the Lord, for his love endures forever.'"

—2 CHRONICLES 20:21-22

THERE IS SOMETHING PROFOUNDLY powerful about worship. In a world filled with distractions, chaos, and battles—both external and internal—worship has the ability to center us, to remind us who God is, and to realign our hearts to His truth. But more than that, worship can be a weapon. It is a force that cuts through the confusion of the enemy's lies and brings forth the truth of God's sovereignty.

Worship is a divine weapon in the hands of believers, capable of shifting atmospheres, altering situations, and defeating spiritual enemies. The concept of worship as a weapon is vividly displayed in the biblical account of King Jehoshaphat in 2 Chronicles 20. Here, we see an extraordinary example of how worship can lead to victory on the battlefield—both physical and spiritual.

We will explore how worship, when wielded in faith, can become a mighty tool in spiritual warfare. We will examine key biblical stories, such as that of Jehoshaphat, and reflect on the spiritual implications of worship in our lives today. As believers, we are engaged in a daily battle, not against flesh and blood, but against the spiritual forces of evil in the heavenly realms (Ephesians 6:12). Worship is one of the most powerful weapons God has given us to stand firm and gain victory in this battle.

The story of Jehoshaphat found in 2 Chronicles 20 is a compelling narrative of faith, worship, and divine intervention. Jehoshaphat, the king of Judah, faced an overwhelming military threat. A vast army composed of the Moabites, Ammonites, and Meunites was marching against Judah. In the face of such an imposing enemy, fear would have been a natural response, yet Jehoshaphat did something extraordinary—he turned to God.

The first act of this story is Jehoshaphat's humility and reliance on God. Rather than relying on military strategy, political alliances, or his own strength, Jehoshaphat sought the Lord. He called a national fast and gathered the people of Judah to seek God's help. In his prayer, he acknowledged the Lord's sovereignty and reminded God of His promises to protect His people (2 Chronicles 20:6-12).

Jehoshaphat's faith was bold. In response to his prayer, a prophet named Jahaziel delivered a message from God: *"Do not be afraid or discouraged because of this vast army. For the battle is **not yours, but God's"** (2 Chronicles 20:15). The instructions given were astonishing. God told them not to fight but to stand firm and watch the deliverance He would bring. How would God accomplish this victory? Through worship.

Jehoshaphat appointed men to sing and praise God, placing them at the front of the army. This was an unconventional strategy, to say the least. Can you imagine being a soldier on that battlefield, armed with weapons, watching a choir lead the charge? From a purely military standpoint, this decision seemed absurd. But from a spiritual standpoint, it was an act of profound faith. Jehoshaphat understood that victory would come, not by human might, but by the power of God—and worship was the key to unlocking that power.

As they began to sing and praise, the Lord set ambushes against their enemies. Confusion spread through the enemy camp, and the armies that had come to destroy Judah ended up destroying one another. Not a single enemy soldier remained, and the people of Judah did not have to lift a sword. Victory was won through the power of worship.

A Strategic Approach to Spiritual Warfare

Jehoshaphat's story illustrates a vital truth: worship is not just a response to victory; it can be the cause of victory. In spiritual warfare, worship is one of the most potent weapons we possess. But how exactly does worship function as a weapon?

1. **Worship Declares God's Sovereignty**

   When we worship, we proclaim the greatness of God. We declare His sovereignty over our circumstances, our struggles, and our enemies. In doing so, we remind ourselves and the spiritual realm that God is in control. The enemy operates through deception, often attempting to magnify our problems and minimize God's power. Worship flips that script. It puts our focus on God's infinite power, not the size of the challenge before us.

2. **Worship Shifts the Atmosphere**

   Worship changes the spiritual atmosphere. In moments of worship, God's presence is tangibly felt. In the book of Psalms, we are told that God inhabits the praises of His people (Psalm 22:3). When we worship, we invite the presence of God into our situation. His presence brings peace, clarity, and strength, and it dispels fear and confusion. Just as God's presence led to the destruction of Judah's enemies, so too can His presence bring down the spiritual strongholds in our lives.

3. **Worship Builds Faith**

   Worship is an act of faith. When we worship in the midst of adversity, we are declaring our trust in God, even when the outcome is uncertain. Worship strengthens our faith because it refocuses our attention on God's character and His promises. As our faith is strengthened, we are better equipped to stand firm in spiritual battles. Jehoshaphat's decision to send worshipers ahead of the army was a radical act of faith. He trusted that God's word was true and that worship would lead to victory—and it did.

4. Worship Silences the Enemy

There is a spiritual principle that is often overlooked: worship silences the enemy. In Psalm 8:2, we read, *"Through the praise of children and infants you have established a stronghold against your enemies, to silence the foe and the avenger."* When we worship, we silence the lies and accusations of the enemy. Satan seeks to undermine our faith, sow seeds of doubt, and convince us that God is not for us. But worship drowns out his voice. It amplifies the truth of who God is and what He has done, leaving no room for the enemy's deceptions.

5. Worship Is a Posture of Surrender

At its core, worship is an act of surrender. It is a recognition that we are not in control and that we need God to intervene. In spiritual warfare, surrender to God is often the key to victory. As we humble ourselves in worship, we align our hearts with God's will and allow Him to fight on our behalf. Jehoshaphat's prayer of surrender set the stage for Judah's deliverance. He acknowledged his own inability to win the battle and placed his trust entirely in God's hands. Worship is a way of surrendering our battles to God and trusting that He will fight for us.

Worship in the Midst of Adversity

We may not face physical armies in our daily lives, but we are certainly engaged in a spiritual battle. The Bible is clear that our enemy, Satan, is constantly seeking to devour us (1 Peter 5:8). Whether through temptation, discouragement, fear, or doubt, the enemy's goal is to separate us from God and weaken our faith. Yet, as believers, we have been given divine weapons to combat these spiritual attacks, and worship is one of the most powerful.

Every day, we wake up to a spiritual battlefield. The enemy is relentless in his pursuit to steal, kill, and destroy (John 10:10). But we do not fight this battle alone, nor do we fight it in our own strength. Worship is a weapon we can wield daily to push back against the enemy's advances.

In moments of fear, we can worship to remind ourselves that God is our refuge and strength (Psalm 46:1). In times of temptation, we can worship to declare that God is greater than the fleeting pleasures of sin. In seasons of doubt, we can worship to proclaim that God is faithful and His promises are true.

One of the most powerful aspects of worship is that it shifts our focus. When we are in the midst of adversity, it is easy to become consumed by our problems. But worship lifts our eyes off our circumstances and places them on God. It reminds us that, no matter what we are facing, God is bigger, God is stronger, and God is with us.

Worship in My Own Battles

As a military man who served 21 years in the Navy, I understand the significance of strategy, preparation, and strength on the battlefield. But over the years, I have come to realize that some battles cannot be won with physical strength or tactical intelligence. There are battles that are fought in the heart and the mind—battles that require spiritual weapons.

There have been moments in my life when the enemy's attacks felt overwhelming. Times when fear, doubt, or discouragement threatened to overtake me. Yet in those moments, I discovered the power of worship. When I turned to God in praise, even when my circumstances hadn't changed, I found peace. I found strength. And I found victory.

Worship has become a vital part of my spiritual arsenal. It is not just something I do on Sunday mornings; it is a daily practice that helps me stay grounded in God's truth and prepared for the battles I face. Whether I am praising God in the midst of a storm or worshiping Him in times of peace, I know that worship is a weapon that has the power to change my circumstances and strengthen my faith.

Worship is a powerful weapon in the hands of believers. It has the ability to bring down strongholds, silence the enemy, and lead us to victory. Jehoshaphat's story is a vivid reminder that when we place our trust in God and engage in worship, we can experience His miraculous intervention in our lives.

As you engage in your own spiritual battles, I encourage you to make worship a central part of your strategy. When the enemy comes against you with fear, doubt, or discouragement, lift your voice in praise. Declare the greatness of God. Remind yourself of His promises. And trust that, just as He fought for Judah, He will fight for you.

Worship is not just a response to victory; it is a means to victory. So, let us raise a hallelujah, even in the midst of the storm. Let us worship with faith, knowing that our God is mighty, and He will deliver us from every enemy that comes against us. For the battle is not ours; it is the Lord's.

Chapter 4: Humility and Worship

A Journey of Surrender

"He has shown you, O mortal, what is good. And what does the Lord require of you? To act justly, to love mercy, and to walk humbly with your God."

—MICAH 6:8

AS WE BEGIN TO explore what it truly means to worship with humility, I want to start with a moment of reflection—a moment that brought me face to face with the reality of how small I really am in the grand scheme of things.

In the military, we're encouraged to keep detailed records of our careers. For years, I kept everything in what we called an "I Love Me" binder—a two-inch, three-ring binder that held my evaluations, training certificates, and awards. This little binder told the story of my 22-year career in the Navy. It was my life on paper—every promotion, every accolade, every hard-earned milestone—compressed into that small, tidy space.

As I began preparing for retirement, I couldn't help but flip through those pages. And as I did, a strange feeling settled in. Everything I had poured myself into for over two decades could be held in my hands. There was something humbling—almost jarring—about that realization. It made me step back and ask: *What really matters?* What legacy was I truly leaving behind?

That's when God began to show me something deeper—true humility isn't about thinking less of yourself, but about recognizing who you are in light of who He is. Worship, at its core, begins with that recognition. It's not about our titles, achievements, or even our sacrifices. Worship with humility means coming before God, stripped of status, aware of our complete dependence on Him, and in awe that the Creator of the universe would even invite us into His presence.

That little binder taught me that what matters most isn't what's written on a piece of paper, but what's written on the heart of someone who bows before the Lord with reverence and surrender. If we're going to worship in spirit and truth, it starts here—with humility.

Humility doesn't come naturally to most of us. In a culture that encourages us to outdo others—whether at work, in sports, or academics—we often find ourselves striving to meet external expectations. Success is often measured by achievements, wealth, or accolades, and the notion of "humbling oneself" is frequently viewed as weakness. Yet, worship calls us to a different standard. It calls us to approach God with humility, to recognize our limitations, and to surrender our pride.

If worship is truly about our relationship with God, then the words of Micah take on a deeply personal significance:

> "He has shown you, O mortal, what is good. And what does the Lord require of you? To act justly, to love mercy, and to walk humbly with your God." (Micah 6:8)

This passage encapsulates the foundation of true surrender. Worshiping God in humility isn't about impressing Him with our deeds or possessions; it is about approaching Him with a heart of submission, recognizing His sovereignty and our dependence on Him.

The journey of worship is a journey of humility. As Jesus described in John 4:23, "Yet a time is coming and has now come when the true worshipers will worship the Father in the Spirit and in truth, for they are the kind of worshipers the Father seeks."

True worship stems from a humble heart that seeks God's presence above all else. If we are to be the worshipers the Father seeks, humility must be at the core of our devotion.

Humility vs. Vanity: The Internal Battle

The tension between humility and vanity is an ancient battle, fought in the hearts of all who seek to follow God. Vanity tells us that we can earn our place before God through our achievements, wealth, or status. Humility, on the other hand, reminds us that we bring nothing to the table apart from what God has already given us. The world encourages us to build ourselves up, to be proud of our accomplishments, and to seek validation from others, but worship requires a different mindset. It requires the surrender of our pride and the recognition of our smallness before the greatness of God.

A powerful illustration of this tension is found in the story of the Rich Young Ruler, as recorded in Mark 10:17-22. The man approached Jesus, seeking eternal life:

> "As He was setting out on a journey, a man ran up to Him and knelt before Him, and asked Him, 'Good Teacher, what shall I do so that I may inherit eternal life?' But Jesus said to him, 'Why do you call Me good? No one is good except God alone. You know the commandments: "Do not murder, Do not commit adultery, Do not steal, Do not give false testimony, Do not defraud, Honor your father and mother."' And he said to Him, 'Teacher, I have kept all these things from my youth.' Looking at him, Jesus showed love to him and said to him, 'One thing you lack: go and sell all you possess and give to the poor, and you will have treasure in heaven; and come, follow Me.' But he was deeply dismayed by these words, and he went away grieving; for he was one who owned much property."

This story captures the essence of the battle between humility and vanity. The rich young ruler approached Jesus with a desire to inherit eternal life, but his wealth stood in the way of his total surrender. He had followed the commandments, yet he lacked the humility to part with his riches and trust in God's provision. His pride was inextricably tied to his possessions, and when faced with the choice between following Christ and holding onto his wealth, he chose the latter.

Like the rich young ruler, many of us find ourselves caught between who we are and who Christ calls us to be. The world tells us to cling to our status, our possessions, and our self-made identities, but Christ invites us to lay it all down in humble worship. The battle between humility and vanity is not merely about money—it's about anything that stands in the way of our dependence on God.

The Humbling Power of Surrender

For the rich young ruler, it was wealth that prevented his full surrender to God. But for many of us, the obstacles might be different. Perhaps it's the illusion of control over our own lives, the comfort of routine, or the fear of stepping into the unknown where God might be leading us. Humility demands that we surrender not only our external possessions but also our internal desires for power, control, and autonomy.

Humility is not about self-deprecation or thinking less of ourselves; rather, it is about thinking rightly of ourselves in relation to God. It's about recognizing our limitations and trusting in God's infinite wisdom and provision. The Apostle Paul reminds us of this truth in Philippians 4:6-7, where he writes:

> "Do not be anxious about anything, but in every situation, by prayer and petition, with thanksgiving, present your requests to God. And the peace of God, which transcends all understanding, will guard your hearts and your minds in Christ Jesus."

When we walk humbly with God, we release the burden of trying to control every aspect of our lives. In humility, we acknowledge that God is in control and that His plans are far greater than our own. As we surrender to Him, we begin to experience the peace that comes from relying on the One who is sovereign over all.

The Ultimate Example of Humility: Jesus Christ

If we are ever unsure of what humility looks like in worship, we need only look to Jesus Christ, who embodied humility in every aspect of His life and ministry. Though He was God, He did not cling to His divine privileges. Instead, He chose to humble Himself and take on the form of a servant, becoming obedient to the point of death on a cross.

In Philippians 2:5-8, Paul captures the humility of Christ with these words:

> "Indeed, let this attitude be in you, which was also in Christ Jesus. Though He was by nature God, He did not consider equality with God as a prize to be displayed, but He emptied Himself by taking the nature of a servant. When He was born in human likeness, and His appearance was like that of any other man, He humbled Himself by becoming obedient to death—even death on a cross."

Let that sink in: Jesus, the Son of God, humbled Himself as a servant. The King of Kings descended from heaven to serve humanity, demonstrating what it means to worship God with a humble heart. If anyone had the right to exalt themselves, it was Jesus, yet He chose the path of humility, becoming the ultimate example of surrender in worship.

One of the most poignant examples of Christ's humility is found in John 13, where Jesus washes the feet of His disciples. In the ancient world, foot-washing was a task reserved for the lowest of servants, yet Jesus willingly took on this role to serve His disciples. As He washed their feet, He demonstrated that true leadership and worship are rooted in humility and servanthood. Afterward, He said to them:

> "Do you understand what I have done for you? You call me 'Teacher' and 'Lord,' and rightly so, for that is what I am.

Now that I, your Lord and Teacher, have washed your feet,
you also should wash one another's feet. I have set you an
example that you should do as I have done for you." (John
13:12-15)

This act of service was not merely a lesson in humility; it
was a powerful demonstration of what it means to worship God
by serving others. In washing His disciples' feet, Jesus was showing them that worship is not just about what happens in the
temple or synagogue—it's about how we live our lives in humble
service to others.

The Path of Humility: A Daily Surrender

Humility is not a one-time decision; it is a daily act of surrender.
Each day, we must choose to lay down our pride, our desires, and
our ambitions in order to follow Christ more closely. The rich
young ruler couldn't make this choice, but we are called to something different. We are called to follow Christ's example of humble
surrender, knowing that it is in our weakness that His strength is
made perfect (2 Corinthians 12:9).

In the same way that Jesus surrendered His will to the Father,
we too are invited to surrender our will in worship. This daily act
of surrender may look different for each of us. For some, it may
mean letting go of control over our future; for others, it may mean
stepping out of our comfort zone to serve in ways that stretch us.
Whatever it is, true worship requires humility—a willingness to
say, "Not my will, but Yours be done."

Humility is at the heart of true worship. As we lay down
our pride and surrender our lives to God, we open ourselves to a
deeper relationship with Him. The journey of worship is a journey of humility, one that requires us to trust in God's provision
and follow the example of Christ, who humbled Himself to the
point of death.

In our worship, may we seek to walk humbly with our God,
trusting in His goodness and grace. Just as Micah 6:8 reminds
us, God has shown us what is good: to act justly, love mercy, and

walk humbly with Him. Let us embrace this path of humility, knowing that it is in our surrender that we find true freedom and joy in worship.

As we continue to grow in our worship journey, may we strive to be the kind of worshipers the Father seeks—those who worship in spirit and in truth, with hearts of humility.

Chapter 5: **Worship Through Obedience**

"If you love me, keep my commands"

—JOHN 14:15

HAVE YOU EVER FOUND yourself in a situation where you didn't follow instructions completely and later regretted it? I know I have. Growing up under the watchful eye of a single mother, I learned quickly that not following her orders to the letter would lead to consequences. I was free to make my own choices, but I have to accept the consequences too,". That stayed with me, especially when I faced the results of my disobedience. Whether in the form of a missed opportunity, unnecessary hardship, or a broken relationship, the consequences were always present.

King Saul also learned this truth the hard way. When God gives instructions, partial obedience is disobedience. In 1 Samuel 15, we read that Saul was commanded to destroy the Amalekites, leaving nothing behind—people, livestock, and all possessions were to be utterly destroyed as an act of divine judgment. However, Saul spared the Amalekite king, Agag, and kept the best livestock, supposedly to offer sacrifices to the Lord. When confronted by the prophet Samuel, Saul defended his actions, claiming that his motives were pure, and that he had saved the best of the spoils to honor God. But Samuel's response was direct and unyielding:

"Does the Lord delight in burnt offerings and sacrifices as much as in obeying the Lord? To obey is better than sacrifice, and to heed is better than the fat of rams. For rebellion is like the sin of divination, and arrogance like the evil of idolatry. Because you have rejected the word of the Lord, he has rejected you as king" (1 Samuel 15:22-23, NIV).

This response from God's prophet should make every believer pause and reflect. What does this tell us about the nature of worship and obedience? It reveals that God is more concerned with our willingness to follow His commands than with any external act of worship we might offer. In other words, obedience is the highest form of worship. Part of our journey of worship has an inseparable link between worship and obedience, showing that our love for God and our desire to honor Him are best demonstrated by our willingness to listen to His voice and follow His instructions—fully.

The Example of King Saul: The Danger of Rationalizing Disobedience

Saul's story in 1 Samuel 15 is a cautionary tale for every believer. God's command to destroy the Amalekites wasn't just about wiping out a nation; it was a call for absolute obedience. The Amalekites had long opposed Israel, and God had determined that their time of judgment had come. Saul was tasked with executing that judgment, but he allowed human reasoning to interfere with divine instruction. He spared King Agag, perhaps thinking it was more honorable to capture a king than to kill him. He kept the best livestock, possibly assuming that offering sacrifices to God from the spoils would be a noble and acceptable alternative to full obedience.

Saul's actions seemed reasonable by human standards. However, God's standard isn't about what seems reasonable; it's about whether we trust Him enough to obey, even when we don't fully understand His reasoning. Saul's decision to prioritize his own judgment over God's revealed a heart problem. He was more concerned with appearances and immediate benefits than with honoring God's command.

This brings us to a critical point: partial obedience is still disobedience. Saul did most of what God asked, but he left out key details. In our own lives, we might be tempted to justify our actions when we only do part of what God commands. We may rationalize that our intentions are good, or that what we are doing is "close enough." But God's standard doesn't change. His desire is for complete obedience, not half-hearted or conditional adherence to His will.

The Subtle Temptation of Compromise

In our own lives, compromise can be subtle. Maybe God is calling us to let go of certain habits or relationships, but we decide to keep just a little of them, reasoning that it's "not that bad." Or perhaps we feel called to a specific act of service, but we modify it to suit our convenience. Like Saul, we might believe that our good intentions will make up for the areas where we fall short. But God is clear: obedience is better than sacrifice.

When we fail to fully obey, we are effectively placing our judgment above God's. We may not always understand why God asks what He does, but faith means trusting that His ways are higher than ours (Isaiah 55:9). Our obedience is a reflection of our trust in His wisdom and sovereignty.

Obedience as Worship: Aligning Our Hearts with God's Will

At its core, obedience is a matter of the heart. Worship is more than the songs we sing on Sunday or the prayers we offer during our quiet time. Worship is about living a life that is aligned with God's will. Jesus makes this connection clear in John 14:15 when He says, "If you love me, keep my commands." Worship is about loving God, and love, in the biblical sense, is not just a feeling—it's an action.

God desires that our worship be expressed through obedience because it is in obeying Him that we demonstrate our reverence and submission to His authority. When we choose to obey, even when it's difficult or inconvenient, we are offering up a powerful act of worship. This is why Samuel's response to Saul was so profound. The prophet emphasized that God isn't impressed by sacrifices if they are offered in the place of obedience. The outward rituals of worship mean little if the heart behind them is rebellious or indifferent to God's instructions.

Worship and obedience cannot be separated. True worship stems from a heart that seeks to honor God in every aspect of life, not just in formal acts of devotion. As Deuteronomy 10:12-13 reminds us, "And now, Israel, what does the LORD your God ask of you but to fear the LORD your God, to walk in obedience to him, to love him, to serve the LORD your God with all your heart and with all your soul, and to observe the LORD's commands and decrees that I am giving you today for your own good?"

Obedience in Everyday Life

Obedience isn't always about grand gestures; it's about daily faithfulness in the little things. It's about being honest when no one is watching, choosing kindness when it's easier to ignore someone, and following God's call even when it seems impractical. Every act of obedience, no matter how small, is a declaration that we trust God and honor Him above our own desires.

In our worship journey, obedience to God is the highest form of reverence we can offer. When we align our will with His, we are not just performing religious rituals; we are engaging in true, spirit-filled worship. This type of worship transcends words and rituals—it is a living sacrifice, holy and acceptable to God (Romans 12:1).

The Cost of Disobedience: Missing Out on God's Best

Saul's disobedience cost him dearly. God rejected him as king, and his disobedience set in motion a chain of events that ultimately led to his downfall. The principle is clear: when we choose disobedience, we not only dishonor God, but we also miss out on His best for our lives. Obedience opens the door for God's blessings, while disobedience leads to loss and regret.

Obedience is not always easy, but it is always worth it. God's commands are not arbitrary; they are given for our good. When we obey, we position ourselves to receive His blessings, protection, and guidance. Deuteronomy 28 outlines the blessings that come from obedience, as well as the curses that result from disobedience. The stakes are high, but so are the rewards. When we choose to obey, we align ourselves with God's purposes and experience the fullness of life that He intends for us.

Listening to God's Voice

One of the key elements of obedience is the ability to listen to God's voice. Saul failed in this regard because he allowed his own reasoning to overshadow God's clear instruction. In our own lives, it's important to cultivate a heart that is sensitive to God's voice. This requires spending time in His Word, seeking Him in prayer, and being open to the guidance of the Holy Spirit. When we listen carefully, we are better equipped to obey fully.

Obedience is the key to unlocking the fullness of God's plan for our lives. It may not always be easy, but it is always the right choice. Just as Saul's disobedience led to his downfall, our disobedience can prevent us from experiencing the fullness of God's blessings. But when we choose to obey, we honor God and position ourselves to receive His best.

In the end, the story of Saul teaches us a vital lesson: worship and obedience are inseparable. Saul's downfall came not because he failed to offer sacrifices, but because he failed to obey.

His heart was not fully aligned with God's will, and that disobedience cost him everything.

As followers of Christ, we are called to worship God not just with our words or rituals, but with our whole lives. Obedience is the highest form of worship, and it is through our obedience that we demonstrate our love for God. Whether in the small, daily decisions or the big, life-altering choices, our obedience is an act of worship that honors God and invites His blessings into our lives.

In our journey of worship, let us remember the words of Samuel: "To obey is better than sacrifice, and to heed is better than the fat of rams." True worship is found in a heart that is fully submitted to God, a heart that listens for His voice and responds in obedience. May we strive to live lives of worship through our obedience to Him.

Chapter 6: **Worship in the Wilderness**

"He alone is my rock and my salvation, my fortress where I will not be shaken. My victory and honor come from God alone. He is my refuge, a rock where no enemy can reach me."

—PSALM 62:6-7

HAVE YOU EVER BEEN faced with a storm in your life where worshiping God was not even a remote possibility? For me, my darkest moments came when I faced depression—a battle so overwhelming that it felt as though my entire world was closing in around me. In those days, my mental health plummeted to rock bottom. I couldn't see a way out of the pain. I believed that the only way to end the suffering was to end my life. I was desperate for an escape, and I began to search for ways to find a permanent solution to the anguish that gripped my soul.

In that season, the idea of worship was far from my heart. Worship felt like a distant memory, something I couldn't even imagine mustering in the midst of my internal turmoil. I didn't turn to God in worship, and in many ways, I didn't even believe that He could help me in my despair. But now, as I reflect on those moments, I see clearly that it was precisely in that darkness where worship was most needed. Worship is the doorway to hope, and it brings us closer to the Creator when everything else is pulling us away.

In my struggle, I had distanced myself from God. The storm around me had blinded me to the presence of the One who could calm it. I wasn't the first, nor the last, to do this. Often, in the darkest seasons, we believe we have to take control and solve the problems ourselves. However, the act of worship is a surrender—it is an admission that we are not in control, that God holds the power, and that our relationship with Him is what truly matters.

In the Psalms, we see David, a man after God's own heart, cry out in the midst of his own pain and trials. In Psalm 62:6-7, David writes, "He alone is my rock and my salvation, my fortress where I will not be shaken. My victory and honor come from God alone. He is my refuge, a rock where no enemy can reach me." Even in his suffering, David understood that God's steadfastness and salvation were the keys to his survival. Worship allowed David to acknowledge God's presence in his storm, to cling to the one thing that could not be shaken.

Relating to the Israelites in the Wilderness

In the storms of life, we can often find ourselves relating to the Israelites as they fled from Pharaoh's army. When they found themselves between the Red Sea and the approaching enemy, their fear overwhelmed their faith. They did not turn to God in worship; instead, they let their anxiety lead them. They said to Moses in Exodus 14:11-12, "Was it because there were no graves in Egypt that you brought us to the desert to die? What have you done to us by bringing us out of Egypt? Didn't we say to you in Egypt, 'Leave us alone; let us serve the Egyptians'? It would have been better for us to serve the Egyptians than to die in the desert!"

Fear gripped their hearts, and worship was far from their minds. They could not see God's hand moving on their behalf. Yet, God was still there. Even though their fear dominated their thoughts, God had a plan to save them. And after He miraculously parted the Red Sea and delivered them from the Egyptians, their response was one of worship.

Moses and Miriam led the people in a song of praise, declaring, "I will sing to the Lord, for he is highly exalted. Both horse and driver he has hurled into the sea. The Lord is my strength and my defense; he has become my salvation. He is my God, and I will praise him, my father's God, and I will exalt him" (Exodus 15:1-2 NIV).

The beauty of this story is that even though the Israelites were consumed by fear, God still saved them. The storm did not overwhelm them. After their deliverance, their hearts were filled with worship, and they could see God's hand in their situation.

Our Spiritual Journey through the Wilderness

Like the Israelites, we face moments in life where fear, uncertainty, and doubt seem insurmountable. We may find ourselves in situations where it feels like we are trapped between the "Red Sea" and the "enemy" behind us. In these moments, it is easy to give in to fear, to lose our worshipful hearts, just as the Israelites did. But the story of the exodus reminds us that even in the most desperate circumstances, God is still with us, fighting on our behalf.

Worship in the face of fear becomes an act of trust. It's not about waiting until the storm has passed or until we have been delivered from our trials. True worship happens in the midst of the storm, when we trust that God is working for our good, even when we cannot see the way forward. Exodus 14:14 reminds us, "The Lord will fight for you; you need only to be still." This stillness, this act of trusting God, is at the heart of worship in dark times.

When we worship during hardship, we are not simply responding to what God has done, but we are declaring what we believe God will do. It is a statement of faith that, even though we do not see the victory yet, we know that God is in control, and He is worthy of our praise.

Worship as a Declaration of God's Power

Moses and Miriam's song after the parting of the Red Sea reminds us that worship is not just a response to God's provision, but a declaration of His ongoing faithfulness and power. They led the Israelites in a song of praise because they recognized that it was God's strength that had delivered them.

We, too, are called to lift our voices in worship, even in the face of uncertainty. When we worship in difficult times, we proclaim that God is our deliverer, even before we see the evidence of His deliverance. This act of worship becomes a weapon in spiritual warfare. It is a way of reminding ourselves and declaring to the world that God is still on His throne, that He is still powerful, and that He is still working on our behalf.

Worship Shifts Our Focus from Problems to God's Sovereignty

In dark moments, our natural tendency is to fixate on our problems. Fear, pain, and anxiety can dominate our thoughts, pushing us further from God and robbing us of peace. But worship reorients our focus. When we worship, we are reminded that God is greater than our circumstances. Worship is an acknowledgment of God's sovereignty, a reminder that He is still good, even when life feels overwhelming.

Worship also aligns our hearts with God's will. In times of trial, we often try to take control, striving to solve our problems in our own strength. But worship reminds us that God is in control, that His ways are higher than ours, and that His plans are for our good. When we surrender in worship, we soften our hearts and become more receptive to God's guidance and comfort during difficult times.

Furthermore, worship builds resilience in our faith. Worship, especially in challenging seasons, strengthens our spiritual resilience. It is a discipline that anchors us in God's presence, even when life feels chaotic. By choosing to worship, we declare that our faith is not dependent on our circumstances, but on the unchanging character of God. This builds a deep-rooted faith that can endure even the darkest of seasons.

Worship is not just for the mountaintop experiences of life. It is in the valleys, the dark nights of the soul, where worship becomes a lifeline, a way to stay connected to God when everything else feels uncertain. In those moments, we must remind ourselves that worship is a choice—a choice to trust in God's goodness, to believe in His promises, and to find peace in His presence.

Let us learn to worship through the storm, knowing that God is with us, fighting on our behalf, and will ultimately bring us through to the other side. Just as the Israelites praised God after their deliverance, we too will have moments of victory and triumph to celebrate. But until then, we must continue to worship, trusting that God is working all things together for our good.

In every season, let worship be the anchor for our souls, drawing us closer to our Creator and deepening our relationship with Him.

Chapter 7: **Worshiping In All Seasons**

"I will extol the Lord at all times; his praise will always be on my lips. I will glory in the Lord; let the afflicted hear and rejoice."

—PSALM 34:1-2

KING DAVID STANDS AS one of the most revered and complex figures in Scripture—not because he was flawless, but because of his relentless pursuit of God. Referred to as a man after God's own heart (1 Samuel 13:14), David's life reveals a deep devotion that was most evident in his worship.

David's worship was not limited to specific places or occasions. It was a way of life—woven into moments of triumph, sorrow, repentance, and loss. Whether on the battlefield, in the temple, or alone in the wilderness, David consistently turned his heart toward God.

What makes David's worship so compelling is that it transcended circumstances. He celebrated in victory, mourned in grief, and humbled himself in repentance, yet through it all, he never stopped seeking God. His life reminds us that true worship is not defined by our situation but by the posture of our hearts.

Ultimately, David shows us that worship is not a one-time act or reserved for joyful moments—it's a lifelong journey. In every season, through every emotion, David worshiped with honesty and intention, offering us a powerful example of what it means to truly seek God.

David a Worshiper in Victory

Triumphant worship is often the easiest form of worship to engage in. When life is going well, when victories are won, and blessings abound, our hearts naturally overflow with praise and thanksgiving. These are the moments when we feel closest to God, and worship comes easily. David certainly knew how to worship in times of triumph.

One of the most memorable moments of David's triumphant worship was when he brought the Ark of the Covenant to Jerusalem. This was a moment of great spiritual and national significance for Israel, as the Ark symbolized God's presence among His people. David's response to this event was one of overwhelming joy and exuberant worship.

In 1 Chronicles 16, we see David leading the nation in a song of thanks after the Ark is brought into the city:

> "Give thanks to the Lord, call on His name; make known among the nations what He has done. Sing to Him, sing praise to Him; tell of all His wonderful acts." (1 Chronicles 16:8-9)

David's worship was unrestrained. He danced before the Lord with all his might (2 Samuel 6:14), expressing his gratitude and reverence for God's presence. This scene exemplifies the kind of joyful, celebratory worship that naturally follows moments of triumph. David wasn't concerned with appearances or what others thought; his heart was focused solely on glorifying God.

David's example shows us that worship is a fitting response to victory. When we experience success, blessings, or breakthroughs in life, our hearts should overflow with gratitude toward God. Whether it's a professional achievement, a personal milestone, or a spiritual victory, triumph should lead us into worship.

Like David, we should not hold back in expressing our praise and thanks to God during these times. We see this principle reflected even today in moments of public acknowledgment, like when athletes point to the sky after a victory or when someone gives thanks after a significant accomplishment. Triumphant worship is a natural response to God's goodness, and it reminds us that every victory ultimately belongs to Him.

David Worshiping in Lament

While triumphant worship is important, David also teaches us that worship in times of lament is equally vital. Life is not always filled with victories and celebrations. There are times of pain, loss, and suffering, and it is in these seasons that worship can take on a deeper, more vulnerable meaning. David's Psalms are filled with expressions of lament—cries of anguish, fear, and despair, yet they are still acts of worship.

David's Psalms of lament often begin with a cry of pain or desperation but end with a declaration of trust in God's character. For instance, in Psalm 64, David pleads for deliverance from his enemies:

> *"Hear me, my God, as I voice my complaint; protect my life from the threat of the enemy."* (Psalm 64:1)

In Psalm 109, David calls out to God for help against those who have slandered and betrayed him:

> *"But you, Sovereign Lord, help me for your name's sake; out of the goodness of your love, deliver me."* (Psalm 109:21)

These Psalms reveal a raw, honest form of worship. David does not hide his pain from God, nor does he pretend that everything is okay. Instead, he brings his suffering before the Lord, trusting that God will hear and respond. This kind of worship requires vulnerability and faith—it acknowledges that we are dependent on God, even in our most broken moments.

Lamenting worship teaches us that it's okay to be honest with God. We do not have to wait until we feel joyful or confident to worship Him. In fact, some of the most powerful moments of worship occur when we bring our pain, confusion, and grief before God, trusting that He can handle our raw emotions. David's laments show us that worship is not only about praise but also about expressing our deepest struggles before the Lord.

One of the most profound aspects of lamenting worship is its ability to transform our perspective. David's Psalms of lament often begin with cries of distress but end with declarations of hope and trust. For example, Psalm 64 begins with a plea for help but concludes with this affirmation of faith:

> "The righteous will rejoice in the Lord and take refuge in him; all the upright in heart will glory in him!" (Psalm 64:10)

In this way, lament leads David back to a place of trust in God's goodness and sovereignty. Lament is not an end in itself; it is a pathway to deeper faith and greater intimacy with God.

David's Repentant Worship

David's life was not without moral failure, and one of his most infamous moments was his sin with Bathsheba. This event represents a low point in David's life, as he committed both adultery and murder in an attempt to cover up his wrongdoing. However, what sets David apart is his response to his sin. When confronted by the prophet Nathan, David did not deny or minimize his actions. Instead, he immediately turned to God in repentance.

In 2 Samuel 12:13-17, we see David's heartfelt repentance:

> "Then David said to Nathan, 'I have sinned against the Lord.' Nathan replied, 'The Lord has taken away your sin. You are not going to die.'" (2 Samuel 12:13)

David's repentance was not just a feeling of regret; it was a profound act of worship. He acknowledged his sin, took full responsibility for his actions, and sought God's forgiveness. This moment of repentance is beautifully captured in Psalm 51, where David pleads for God's mercy and restoration:

> "Create in me a pure heart, O God, and renew a steadfast spirit within me. Do not cast me from your presence or take your Holy Spirit from me. Restore to me the joy of your salvation and grant me a willing spirit, to sustain me."
> (Psalm 51:10-12)

David's worship during this time of repentance shows us that worship is not limited to times of joy or celebration. It is also found in moments of deep contrition and humility. Repentance is a form of worship that acknowledges our need for God's grace and invites Him to cleanse and renew us.

True repentance, as demonstrated by David, is not simply about feeling bad for our sins. It is about turning back to God with a heart that seeks His forgiveness and restoration. In Psalm 51, David not only confesses his sin but also expresses a desire for transformation—a pure heart and a renewed spirit. This is the essence of repentant worship: it leads us into a deeper relationship with God, where we experience His grace and are made new.

David Worshiping in Loss

Perhaps one of the most difficult aspects of David's worship journey is how he responded to personal tragedy. After David's sin with Bathsheba, their child became gravely ill, and despite David's prayers and fasting, the child eventually died. David's response to this heartbreaking loss is one of the most profound examples of worship in the face of grief.

In 2 Samuel 12:20, we see David's reaction:

> "Then David got up from the ground. After he had washed, put on lotions, and changed his clothes, he went into the house of the Lord and worshiped." (2 Samuel 12:20)

David's decision to worship immediately after the death of his child is both surprising and deeply moving. Even in the midst of his grief, David chose to turn to God in worship. This act of worship demonstrates David's unwavering trust in God, even when his prayers were not answered in the way he had hoped.

Worshiping after loss is perhaps one of the most difficult things to do. When we experience grief, disappointment, or unanswered prayers, it can feel almost impossible to worship. Yet David's example shows us that worship is not dependent on our circumstances. Even in times of profound sorrow, we can still turn to God in worship, trusting that He is with us in our pain.

David's story also teaches us that unanswered prayers do not negate God's goodness. While David's prayers for his child were not answered in the way he desired, he still chose to worship, recognizing that God's ways are higher than our own. Worship in the midst of loss is an act of surrender, as we trust that God's plan is greater than our understanding.

David's life shows us that worship is not confined to any one season. It encompasses moments of triumph, lament, repentance, and loss. Through it all, David's heart remained anchored in his relationship with God. His worship was not a performance; it was the outflow of a heart that sought after God, no matter the circumstances.

As we walk through our own worship journeys, we would do well to learn from David. Worship is not just about lifting our hands in joy or singing songs of praise in church. It is about bringing all of ourselves—our victories, our failures, our sorrows, and our joys—before God in humble submission. Whether in times of celebration or in the depths of despair, worship is the posture of a heart that continually seeks after God.

David's story reminds us that we are all invited to be worshipers in every season of life. Like David, we can be people after God's own heart, not because we are perfect, but because we always return to Him in worship.

Chapter 8: **Strength in Numbers**

Worship in Community

"And they devoted themselves to the apostles' teaching and the fellowship, to the breaking of bread and the prayers. And awe came upon every soul, and many wonders and signs were being done through the apostles. And all who believed were together and had all things in common."

—ACT 2:42-44

AS A MEMBER OF the Church of Christ, I have grown accustomed to a worship style that relies solely on the human voice. In our tradition, instruments are absent from our services, and the human voice becomes the sole medium of musical expression. This form of worship is not merely a preference but a deeply spiritual experience. There is something undeniably powerful about a congregation of voices, lifting up songs in one accord, without the distractions or embellishments of instruments. Each voice, whether strong or weak, trained or untrained, blends together in harmony, creating a sacred atmosphere. This collective offering of praise has a profound impact, not just on the individuals participating, but on the body as a whole.

The beauty of a cappella worship lies not only in its simplicity but also in its ability to foster unity. When we sing together, we align ourselves in purpose and spirit. Our hearts and minds are tuned to the same pitch, so to speak, as we focus solely on worshiping God. In a world where we are often bombarded with distractions, corporate singing in this way becomes a refuge. It reminds us that worship is not a performance but a collective outpouring of devotion to the Creator.

However, as much as this practice has shaped my spiritual life, I have come to realize that our understanding of corporate worship can sometimes be too limited. We often associate worship with the specific act of gathering in a church building, singing songs, and participating in a formal service. While these are certainly vital aspects of worship, they are not the entirety of it. As we continue to journey together through the subject of worship in this book, we have seen that worship is far more than a place we go or an event we attend. Worship is a way of life. It encompasses every moment of our existence as we live in obedience to God, offering our bodies as living sacrifices (Romans 12:1).

The Church: A Community, Not a Building

When Christ established His church over two millennia ago, He did not construct a building. Instead, He built a community of believers. The church is not a physical structure made of brick and mortar; it is the people who profess faith in Christ. This is a foundational truth that we see throughout the New Testament, especially in the book of Acts.

In Acts 2:42-44, we find a powerful description of the early church:

> *"And they devoted themselves to the apostles' teaching and the fellowship, to the breaking of bread and the prayers. And awe came upon every soul, and many wonders and signs were being done through the apostles. And all who believed were together and had all things in common."*

Here, we see the early believers coming together in a spirit of unity and mutual support. Their worship extended beyond formal gatherings and into their everyday lives as they shared meals, prayed together, and took care of one another's needs.

The early church was a living, breathing community, bound together by a common faith in Christ. This is something we must not lose sight of in our modern context. Too often, we equate "church" with the building we meet in once or twice a week. But the church, as Christ intended it, is much more than that. It is a family of believers who are committed to supporting one another, growing together, and living out the teachings of Christ in every aspect of life.

Equation of Community

The passage from Acts paints a vivid picture of how Christ intended His church to function as a community. In the modern church, however, we sometimes struggle to realize the depth of what this means. What does it look like to be a truly unified, supportive, and growing community in Christ?

1. Unified in Christ

   First and foremost, the church is meant to be unified in Christ. Acts 2:44 tells us that "all who believed were together and had all things in common." This doesn't mean that they were identical in every way or that they agreed on every single issue. Rather, their unity was rooted in their shared faith in Christ. The concept of a unified body is what composes the church, not the physical building.

   Unity in the church is a reflection of the nature of God Himself, who exists in perfect unity as Father, Son, and Holy Spirit. As believers, we are called to reflect that unity in our relationships with one another. This doesn't mean that we ignore differences or pretend that conflicts don't exist. Instead, it means that we prioritize our shared identity in Christ above all else.

2. Supporting One Another

In addition to being unified, the early church was marked by a deep commitment to supporting one another. In Acts 2:46, we read that "day by day, attending the temple together and breaking bread in their homes, they received their food with glad and generous hearts." This passage highlights the fact that the early believers shared their lives with one another. They didn't just meet for a few hours on Sunday morning and then go their separate ways. Instead, they were deeply involved in each other's lives, offering both spiritual and practical support.

This principle of mutual support is just as relevant today as it was in the first century. Whether our blessings are financial, emotional, or spiritual, they are meant to be shared with others. Sometimes, the gifts we have to offer are not monetary but spiritual. We may be called to offer encouragement, wisdom, or simply a listening ear to those who are struggling.

3. Equals Growth

As I was working on this chapter, I couldn't help but think about math. Now, I'll be the first to admit that I'm not a math genius, and I certainly didn't enjoy the subject in school. But as I reflected on the early church's community, I couldn't help but think of a simple equation: unity + support = growth.

When a church is unified in Christ and committed to supporting one another, it will naturally experience growth. This growth may manifest in numbers, as more people are drawn to the loving and supportive environment of the church. But just as importantly, it will lead to spiritual growth as believers mature in their faith and become more like Christ.

Calibration Check: Is Your Church Unified?

At this point, it's worth asking ourselves a few important questions: Is your church unified in Christ? Is your community a place where believers support one another and grow together in their faith? If the answer to any of these questions is unclear, then it may be time to examine the health of your church community.

In many cases, a lack of unity or support within the church is not the result of malicious intent. More often, it's a result of complacency. Over time, we can become so accustomed to the routines and traditions of church life that we forget the true purpose of our gatherings. We may attend services out of habit, but our hearts are not fully engaged. This is why it's important to regularly recalibrate, to ensure that we are aligned with the biblical model of community.

Recalibrate: Correcting the Course

If your church community is not functioning as it should, don't despair. The beauty of the church is that it is built on the foundation of Christ, and His Word provides us with the instructions we need to recalibrate. Often, the changes required are not drastic but rather gentle corrections that help us realign with the biblical framework.

How to Recalibrate a Church

The first step in recalibrating a church is to examine its foundation. Is the church truly built on the teachings of Christ, or has it become more focused on traditions and routines? In my own life, I've experienced times when I needed to recalibrate. During my time in the Navy, I was once placed in a fitness enhancement program because I was over the maximum weight standards. The program required me to participate in daily physical training, and at first, I approached it with a poor attitude. I wasn't giving it my full effort, and one day, the command fitness leader called me out on it.

He said, "I noticed you weren't putting a hundred percent into the workout. You're not cheating me; you're cheating yourself."

That moment stuck with me because it highlighted the importance of being honest with myself. In the same way, when we examine the foundation of our church, we need to be honest. Is our foundation truly in Christ, or have we become so comfortable with our routines that we have begun to turn away from Him? This kind of self-reflection is crucial if we want to recalibrate our church community and get back on track.

Is the Church Unified Under the Banner of Christ?

Once we have examined the foundation, the next step is to ensure that the church is unified. Unity is essential for the health of any church, but it's important to understand that unity does not mean uniformity. It's not about everyone being the same or agreeing on every issue. Instead, unity is about embracing diversity while being bonded by a common faith in Christ.

In the same way that different voices blend together in a cappella music to create harmony, a unified church is composed of individuals with unique gifts, perspectives, and backgrounds who come together for a greater purpose. This sense of togetherness is what allows the church to function as the body of Christ. It's a reflection of the unity that exists within the Trinity—Father, Son, and Holy Spirit working together in perfect harmony.

The Essence of Unity

Unity in the church can be broken down into several key elements:

1. Shared Purpose: A unified church is one where believers come together for a common cause or mission. In the case of the church, that mission is to glorify God and make disciples of all nations.

2. Cooperation: Unity requires cooperation. It's about individuals and groups supporting one another, working together, and collaborating to achieve something greater than themselves.

3. Harmony: Unity doesn't mean there will never be disagreements, but it does mean that there is a sense of peace and understanding between people, even when they have different perspectives or backgrounds.

4. Inclusivity: A unified church is one that values diversity and strives for a collective identity. Everyone should feel like they belong, regardless of their differences.

As we come to the end of this chapter, let's remember that worship is not confined to a single place or event. True worship is lived out in the context of community, where believers are unified in Christ, supporting one another, and growing together in faith. When we embrace the biblical model of community, our worship becomes a powerful testimony to the world of God's love and grace.

In the end, the strength of the church lies in its unity. As we worship together, let us remember the words of Jesus in John 17:21: "That they may all be one, just as you, Father, are in me, and I in you, that they also may be in us, so that the world may believe that you have sent me." Let us strive to be a community that reflects the unity of Christ, supporting one another and growing together in love and faith.

Chapter 9: Worship Through Song and Praise

"Praise the LORD. Praise God in his sanctuary; praise him in his mighty heavens. Praise him for his acts of power; praise him for his surpassing greatness .Praise him with the sounding of the trumpet, praise him with the harp and lyre praise him with timbrel and dancing, praise him with the strings and pipe, praise him with the clash of cymbals, praise him with resounding cymbals. Let everything that has breath praise the LORD. Praise the LORD."

—PSALM 150

MUSIC HAS A WAY of touching the soul in ways words alone often cannot. Across cultures and throughout history, song has served as a powerful expression of joy, lament, celebration, and even defiance. For believers, music carries an even deeper significance—it is a sacred pathway to connect with the divine. There is something uniquely powerful about how a melody can stir the heart, awaken the spirit, and lift the soul to worship God in spirit and in truth. In fact, as I was editing this chapter, a new song by CeCe Winans titled *Come Jesus Come* began to play. All I could do was sit there, tears streaming, in awe of the glory of Christ Jesus.

Paul's words in *Ephesians 5:19* encourage us to "speak to one another with psalms, hymns, and songs from the Spirit. Sing and make music from your heart to the Lord." In these words lies a profound truth: worship through song is not merely a part of our faith—it is a reflection of our heart's posture toward God. Music is more than an activity or a cultural expression; it is a deeply spiritual practice that draws us closer to God and aligns our hearts with His purposes.

The significance of music and song in worship runs like a golden thread through the entire Bible, from the dawn of creation to the final chorus in Revelation. This chapter explores the biblical foundations of worship through music, the spiritual power it holds, and the ways in which it enriches our personal and corporate relationship with God.

The first time I remember being moved by worship through song, I was a teenager at a youth conference. Those in attendance sang with such passion that it seemed to shake the very walls. Their voices weren't polished, and many were off-key, but there was something unmistakable in the atmosphere: God was present. It wasn't the music itself, but the sincerity of their hearts poured out in song.

Music is God's gift to humanity, a language that transcends words and allows us to express what mere language cannot. From the very beginning of creation, music has been a part of God's design. In the book of Job, God describes the dawn of creation in poetic terms, saying that "the morning stars sang together, and all the sons of God shouted for joy" (Job 38:7). This poetic imagery suggests that music was present when the foundations of the world were laid, woven into the fabric of existence as an act of divine worship.

Throughout history, music has served as a bridge between heaven and earth. It carries the power to uplift the downtrodden, to embolden the weak, and to inspire the faithful. In worship, it becomes more than an art form—it becomes a means of encountering the living God.

Biblical Foundations of Worship Through Music

The Bible is filled with examples of God's people using music as a form of worship. From the Psalms of David to the hymns sung by the early church, music has always been a central means of expressing love and reverence for God.

Old Testament Examples

In the Old Testament, music was a vital component of worship, deeply integrated into the spiritual life of Israel. The Book of Psalms, often referred to as the hymnal of ancient Israel, provides countless examples of how music was used to glorify God, confess sins, express gratitude, and even lament suffering. These songs of worship reveal the full spectrum of human emotion, from uncontainable joy to heart-wrenching sorrow.

Take, for instance, *Psalm 95*, where the psalmist declares, "Come, let us sing for joy to the Lord; let us shout aloud to the Rock of our salvation. Let us come before him with thanksgiving and extol him with music and song." These words invite the worshiper to approach God with a heart full of gratitude, using song as a means of exalting His greatness.

King David, in particular, stands out as a model of a worshiper who embraced music wholeheartedly. His journey as a musician began as a shepherd boy, playing the harp to soothe King Saul's troubled spirit (1 Samuel 16:23). But David's legacy as a worshiper was most evident during his reign as king. In *1 Chronicles 16*, David brings the Ark of the Covenant to Jerusalem and leads the people in a psalm of thanksgiving, singing, "Sing to the Lord, all the earth; proclaim his salvation day after day." He even appointed musicians and singers to serve in the temple, ensuring that music would remain an integral part of Israel's worship.

Music in the Old Testament was not merely a personal expression of devotion—it was also a communal act of worship. When the Israelites crossed the Red Sea, Miriam led the women in a victory song accompanied by tambourines and dancing (Exodus

15:20-21). During the dedication of Solomon's temple, musicians and singers joined together in such unity that "the glory of the Lord filled the temple" (2 Chronicles 5:13-14).

Even the instruments used in worship were carefully chosen and consecrated for God's glory. Psalm 150 gives us a glimpse of this orchestration: "Praise him with the sounding of the trumpet, praise him with the harp and lyre, praise him with timbrel and dancing, praise him with the strings and pipe, praise him with the clash of cymbals." Each instrument added its voice to the symphony of praise, creating a sound that was not just heard but felt—a sound that brought heaven and earth into harmony.

New Testament Guidance

The New Testament builds on the rich tradition of worship through music, emphasizing its role in the life of the church. Paul's letters are especially instructive in this regard. In Colossians 3:16, he writes, "Let the message of Christ dwell among you richly as you teach and admonish one another with all wisdom through psalms, hymns, and songs from the Spirit, singing to God with gratitude in your hearts." Here, Paul highlights the multifaceted purpose of music in worship: it is a means of teaching, a tool for encouragement, and an expression of thanksgiving.

Ephesians 5:19 echoes this sentiment, urging believers to "speak to one another with psalms, hymns, and songs from the Spirit. Sing and make music from your heart to the Lord." These passages remind us that worship through music is not about performance or perfection—it is about sincerity and connection. The act of singing is as much for the edification of others as it is for the glorification of God.

One of the most remarkable examples of worship through music in the New Testament comes from the early church. After being imprisoned for their faith, Paul and Silas began to pray and sing hymns to God. Despite their circumstances, they lifted their voices in praise, and their worship had a profound effect. Not only did an earthquake miraculously free them from their chains, but their captor, the jailer, was so moved that he and his entire household came to faith in Christ (Acts 16:25-34).

The Spiritual Power of Singing

Singing holds a unique and irreplaceable spiritual power. It transcends intellect, engaging both heart and spirit, and creates an atmosphere where heaven meets earth. It is not merely an outward act but a deeply spiritual experience that allows believers to encounter God in profound ways. When we sing, we declare truths about God, reinforce our faith, and invite His presence into our midst.

One of the most compelling aspects of singing is its ability to express love and reverence for God. While prayer is a direct conversation with God and reading Scripture provides us with His Word, singing allows us to combine these elements into an act of pure worship. When we sing to God, we are declaring His worthiness, recounting His deeds, and offering our hearts in gratitude.

In Psalm 147:1, the psalmist declares, "How good it is to sing praises to our God, how pleasant and fitting to praise Him!" This verse reveals the inherent goodness and rightness of praising God through song. It is fitting because God is deserving of all worship, and it is pleasant because it brings joy to both the worshiper and the One being worshiped. Singing enables us to pour out our hearts to God in ways that spoken words alone cannot achieve.

Singing is not just an act of worship—it is also a weapon in spiritual warfare. Throughout Scripture, we see how worship through song becomes a tool for overcoming adversity and claiming victory in the name of the Lord.

The story of Jehoshaphat in 2 Chronicles 20 illustrates this truth powerfully. Facing an overwhelming army, King Jehoshaphat turned to God in prayer and was instructed to appoint singers to lead the troops into battle. These singers didn't carry weapons; they carried a song of praise: "Give thanks to the Lord, for His love endures forever." As they sang, the Lord caused confusion among their enemies, and the Israelites achieved victory without lifting a sword. This remarkable story demonstrates that when we worship God, we are inviting His power to intervene on our behalf.

Another profound example of worship as spiritual warfare is found in the story of Paul and Silas in Acts 16. After being beaten and imprisoned for their faith, they chose to worship God by singing hymns in their jail cell. Their worship was an act of defiance against despair, a declaration that God was still in control despite their circumstances. As they sang, a violent earthquake shook the prison, opening the doors and loosening their chains. Their praise not only brought about a miraculous deliverance but also led to the salvation of the jailer and his household. This story reminds us that worship has the power to break chains—both physical and spiritual.

One of the most beautiful aspects of singing in worship is its ability to unite believers. Music has a way of breaking down barriers, creating a shared experience that transcends differences. When we sing together as a congregation, we are reminded that we are part of a larger body, united in our faith and devotion to God.

Paul's words in Ephesians 5:19 emphasize the communal nature of worship through song: "Speak to one another with psalms, hymns, and songs from the Spirit. Sing and make music from your heart to the Lord." Singing is both horizontal and vertical—it is directed toward God but also serves to encourage and uplift fellow believers.

Corporate worship through music fosters a sense of belonging and strengthens the bond between believers. It reminds us that we are not alone in our journey of faith. Whether it's the shared experience of singing a beloved hymn or the energy of a new worship song, music has the power to bring people together and create a sense of unity that reflects the heart of God.

Living Out Worship Through Song

Worship through song is not confined to Sunday mornings—it is a lifestyle. When we embrace music as an integral part of our worship, it becomes a natural extension of our daily walk with God.

Whether we are singing in the quiet of our homes, in the midst of a congregation, or even in the face of trials, music can be a constant source of encouragement and connection with God.

In personal worship, singing allows us to draw near to God in intimate moments of devotion. There is something deeply personal about singing to God in solitude, without the need for an audience or the pressure to perform. It is a time to be vulnerable, to pour out our hearts to Him, and to experience His presence in a profound way. Many believers find that singing during their personal prayer or Bible study time enhances their connection with God, making their worship more heartfelt and meaningful.

Corporate worship, on the other hand, offers the opportunity to join with others in a shared expression of faith. There is a unique power in the collective voices of a congregation lifting up praise to God. This is not just about the sound but about the unity of purpose and the shared desire to glorify God. Singing together reminds us of our identity as members of the body of Christ and strengthens our sense of community.

Singing can also be a way of encouraging others in their faith. Sharing a song that has been meaningful to you or teaching your children to sing worship songs can have a lasting impact. It is a way of passing down the faith and ensuring that the next generation understands the value of worship through music.

A Lifestyle of Praise

As believers, we are called to live lives of worship, and singing is one of the most joyful and powerful ways to fulfill that calling. It is an expression of love, a declaration of faith, and a tool for spiritual transformation. Whether we are singing alone in our rooms, joining our voices with a congregation, or lifting up a song in the midst of trials, our worship through music is a reflection of our heart's devotion to God.

Worship through song is not limited to the sanctuary—it extends into every area of our lives. It is a song that continues even when the music stops, a melody that lingers in our hearts and shapes our actions. As long as there is breath in our lungs, let us use it to sing praises to the Lord.

The words of Psalm 150 serve as a fitting conclusion:

> "Let everything that has breath praise the Lord. Praise the Lord."

With every note we sing, let us offer our hearts to God in gratitude and reverence. For in worship through song, we find not only a way to honor Him but also a way to be transformed by His presence.

Chapter 10: **Worship and Sacrifice**

"Through Jesus, therefore, let us continually offer to God a sacrifice of praise—the fruit of lips that openly profess his name."

—HEBREWS 13:15

THE WORD *SACRIFICE* OFTEN stirs a sense of solemnity and purpose in those who hear it. As a Navy veteran, I understand the cost of sacrifice in a tangible, physical way. For two decades, I watched sailors give their all—sometimes their lives—for the greater good. I felt the loss of shipmates I knew and held dearly. I felt the sting of loved ones who suffered when I was deployed. Yet the greatest lesson I learned wasn't in a uniform but in my faith. The sacrifices God calls us to make as followers of Christ often come in moments of personal pain, challenge, or uncertainty. These sacrifices are acts of worship, moments when we lay our trust, our praise, and even our tears at His feet.

Hebrews 13:15 speaks to this truth: *"Through Jesus, therefore, let us continually offer to God a sacrifice of praise—the fruit of lips that openly profess his name."* The phrase "sacrifice of praise" captures the paradox of worship in hardship. How do we praise when it hurts? How do we sing when we've been silenced by grief? In this step of our journey we will explore what it means to worship in those moments when it feels like you have nothing left to give, but God calls you to offer Him your heart anyway.

Biblical Foundation of Sacrificial Worship

Old Testament Sacrifices as Worship

Sacrificial worship in the Old Testament was a cornerstone of faith. The Levitical system required offerings of animals, grain, and more to demonstrate devotion to God. Each act of sacrifice pointed to something greater than the worshiper—a trust in God's provision and a willingness to obey, even when it cost dearly.

One of the most profound examples of this is Abraham's willingness to sacrifice Isaac (Genesis 22). As a father of four sons, I cannot imagine the turmoil Abraham felt as he walked toward Mount Moriah. Yet his obedience was unwavering because he trusted God to provide. And God did—both in sparing Isaac and in foreshadowing the ultimate sacrifice of His Son, Jesus Christ.

In my own life, I've had moments where God called me to trust Him completely. One such moment was during one Christmas while I was deployed. I could see the pain of those attending the service. As we sang hymns and read Scripture, I could feel their questions and their pain. Yet those moments of worship, offered in the face of personal sacrifice, became some of the most powerful testimonies of faith I've ever witnessed.

New Testament Transition: Spiritual Sacrifices

With Jesus' ultimate sacrifice, the focus of worship shifted from physical offerings to spiritual sacrifices. Romans 12:1 reminds us, *"Therefore, I urge you, brothers and sisters, in view of God's mercy, to offer your bodies as a living sacrifice, holy and pleasing to God— this is your true and proper worship."*

As a worship leader, this verse became a guiding principle for me. Worship wasn't limited to the songs we sang on Sunday mornings—it was reflected in how we lived our lives throughout

A WORSHIPER'S JOURNEY

the week. I often encouraged those I led to view their daily choices—how they treated their coworkers, spoke to their families, and endured life's challenges—as meaningful expressions of worship. The Sacrifice of Praise in Tough Times

The Meaning and Measure of Praise as Sacrifice

The sacrifice of praise isn't about perfection; it's about persistence. It's easy to sing God's praises when life is going well, but the true depth of our worship is revealed when we can lift our voices in the storm. This is the essence of Hebrews 13:15. Worship becomes sacrificial when it costs us something—our comfort, our pride, or even our peace of mind.

When you're standing in the rubble of disappointment, loss, or uncertainty, worship becomes a choice. It's a decision to declare God's goodness, not because of your circumstances but in spite of them. The sacrifice of praise is an act of defiance against despair and doubt. It says, "I trust in God's sovereignty, even when I don't understand His plan."

For me, this lesson became personal during my transition from active duty to civilian life. After 21 years in the Navy, the structured, purposeful rhythm of military service defined my life. Every day had a clear mission; every action contributed to something larger than myself. I wore my uniform with pride, knowing that I was part of a team that made a difference.

But then, retirement came. Suddenly, I was navigating unfamiliar waters. The routines and camaraderie I had relied on for decades were gone. I felt unmoored, unsure of my next steps. My identity as a Navy Chief—something that had shaped me for over two decades—was no longer the anchor it had been.

It was during those moments of uncertainty that I began to understand what it meant to bring a sacrifice of praise. Worship wasn't about how I felt; it was about who God is. Even when I didn't know what the next chapter of my life would look like, I knew that God was faithful.

I remember one morning in particular. I sat at my desk with my Bible open, staring at the words but struggling to focus. My mind was crowded with questions: *What's next? How will I provide for my family? Where is God leading me?* The weight of uncertainty felt crushing. But in that moment, I felt the Spirit nudging me to pray—not for answers, but simply to praise.

So, I did. I began thanking God for His past faithfulness—how He had guided me through deployments, protected my family, and provided opportunities for ministry even in the Navy. I praised Him for His unchanging character: His goodness, His mercy, His sovereignty.

As I worshiped, something shifted in my heart. The circumstances hadn't changed—I still didn't have all the answers—but my perspective did. Worship lifted my eyes off my uncertainty and fixed them on the One who holds the future. That was my sacrifice of praise: choosing to worship in the waiting, in the not-knowing, in the in-between.

In those moments, I realized that worship isn't about the absence of struggle; it's about the presence of God. When we bring a sacrifice of praise, we're declaring that our faith is not dependent on our circumstances. We're saying, "God, You are worthy, even when life feels anything but."

The Cost of the Sacrifice

The sacrifice of praise often demands we surrender things we hold tightly to—our sense of control, our pride, or our comfort. For me, stepping into civilian life required me to relinquish the security I found in my rank and title. It was a humbling process, but it taught me to place my identity fully in Christ.

The Apostle Paul's words in Philippians 4:11–13 took on new meaning for me: *"I have learned to be content whatever the circumstances. I know what it is to be in need, and I know what it is to have plenty. I have learned the secret of being content in any and every situation, whether well fed or hungry, whether living in plenty or in want. I can do all this through Him who gives me strength."*

Paul's contentment didn't come from his external circumstances; it came from his relationship with Christ. This is the heart of the sacrifice of praise. It's not about ignoring our struggles or pretending everything is fine. It's about acknowledging that God is enough, even in the midst of our pain.

Biblical Examples

Job's Worship in Loss

Job 1:20–21 recounts one of the most heart-wrenching acts of worship in Scripture. After losing everything—his children, his wealth, and his livelihood—Job fell to the ground in worship, saying, *"The Lord gave and the Lord has taken away; may the name of the Lord be praised."*

There are few moments more heart-wrenching than standing with families at military funerals. The folded flag, the haunting sound of taps echoing through the still air, and the overwhelming weight of grief pressing on every heart create an atmosphere where time seems to stand still. In those sacred moments, emotions are raw—grief, anger, confusion, pride—all mingling into a quiet storm of sorrow. It's a silence that says everything words cannot.

For many, these ceremonies mark the darkest chapter of their lives. The sight of a uniformed officer kneeling to present the flag "on behalf of a grateful nation" often feels less like an honor and more like a final, unbearable goodbye. The loss is heavy, not only because of who was lost, but because of what they represented—sacrifice, courage, duty, and love.

And yet, even in these depths of despair, something incredible often breaks through: faith. Not loud or boastful, but steady and unshaken. In the tear-streaked faces and trembling hands of parents, spouses, and siblings, there are glimpses of a deeper trust—one that refuses to let go, even when everything else is lost. These are the moments where worship takes on a different form. It isn't a song or a prayer. It's the quiet, courageous choice to say, "I still trust You, God," even when the heart is shattered.

In such moments, true worship is not found in comfort or joy, but in surrender. It is a sacrifice of praise—offered not from abundance, but from brokenness. These are the testimonies that linger long after the final salute, reminders that even in the valley of the shadow of death, faith can still rise.

Paul and Silas in Prison

In Acts 16:25, we find Paul and Silas beaten, shackled, and imprisoned in the innermost part of a Philippian jail. They had been faithful—casting out a spirit from a slave girl and proclaiming the gospel—yet their obedience led to physical suffering and confinement. And yet, the verse says:

> *"About midnight Paul and Silas were praying and singing hymns to God, and the other prisoners were listening to them."*

This moment is more than a display of courage. It is a profound revelation of what worship really is.

Worship, in this context, is not about convenience or atmosphere. There were no instruments, no sanctuary, no freedom of movement. Their backs were likely bleeding, their bodies aching, their futures uncertain. Still, they worshiped. Why?

Because worship is not dependent on circumstance—it is anchored in identity. Paul and Silas weren't praising God because they felt good. They were praising God because He *is* good, even in the middle of their suffering. Their worship was not a reaction to favorable conditions but a declaration of unwavering trust.

In our world today, worship is often associated with music sets, lights, and Sunday morning services. But Paul and Silas challenge us to rethink worship. Their praise at midnight reveals that worship can—and must—rise from the darkest places. It's in the prisons of life—grief, fear, uncertainty, rejection—where our worship carries the most weight.

Worship in hardship becomes a testimony. The other prisoners listened. People notice when praise comes from pain. That kind of worship doesn't just move hearts—it shakes foundations. And that's exactly what happened next: a literal earthquake, doors flinging open, chains loosed. Worship didn't just uplift spirits—it changed circumstances.

For believers today, Acts 16:25 is more than a historical record. It's an invitation. An invitation to worship when we don't feel like it. To sing in the midnight hour. To trust when we can't trace God's hand.

The relational takeaway is this: worship is our response *not to what is happening to us, but to who God is.* And when we choose to worship in the middle of suffering, like Paul and Silas, we not only experience personal breakthrough—we become a witness to those around us.

The Widow's Offering

In Mark 12:41–44, Jesus commends a widow who gives two small coins, noting that she gave more than all the wealthy contributors because she gave out of her poverty. Her act of worship wasn't about the amount but about the heart behind it.

I've seen this kind of faith among military families who would share their belongings, time and money helping other service member's families who just needed help while their Sailor or Marine was deployed. This was more than just sharing blessings, it was sacrificial worship.

Practical Applications for Today

Recognizing Sacrifices in Daily Worship

Worship isn't confined to a church building or limited to Sunday mornings. It happens in the mundane and extraordinary moments of life, woven into our choices, actions, and attitudes.

When my son Landry was deciding to join the Air Force, it became clear to me how worship can take the form of trust and surrender. We had countless conversations about faith, purpose, and the nature of sacrifice. I remember one particular night when we stayed up late, sitting at the kitchen table. Landry asked me, "Dad, how do you know you're making the right choice when you're stepping into something that's new?"

I shared with him my own experiences from the Navy—how stepping into new roles or missions often required faith, not certainty. I encouraged him to pray, seek God's wisdom, and trust that whatever path he chose, God would be with him. As a father, supporting Landry's decision while entrusting his future to God wasn't easy, but it was an act of worship. It was a surrender of my own fears and desires, laying them down before the Lord and trusting Him to guide my son.

Daily sacrifices like these—choosing grace over anger, forgiveness over pride, or trust over worry—are acts of worship. They remind us that every moment of our lives can reflect God's glory if we approach them with a heart surrendered to Him.

Practicing Gratitude in Trials

Gratitude is one of the most powerful forms of sacrificial worship, especially during times of trial. It shifts our focus from our struggles to God's faithfulness, helping us see His hand at work even in the darkest seasons.

I've read and heard about the benefits of keeping a gratitude journal—how listing just a few things each day can shift your mindset. But I'll be honest: I never kept one. Not because I didn't think it was a good idea, but because this practice has always been a struggle for me. In difficult seasons, gratitude didn't come naturally. I found it far easier to focus on what was wrong than to see the small, quiet ways God was still at work.

As I shared earlier, one of the hardest seasons was my transition from active duty to civilian life. The uncertainty of that time was heavy—filled with questions, doubts, and anxiety about the future. And while I didn't document my gratitude in a journal, I had to learn—sometimes painfully—to give thanks anyway. It wasn't always a feeling; it was a choice. I began to find solace in the simple act of saying thank you to God. A quiet moment of prayer, a hug from one of my sons, the steady love of Laura—these became reminders that God was still with me.

Even now, gratitude remains a discipline I have to be intentional about. When I sing hymns with my church family or pray in my study, I make it a point to thank God—not just for the visible blessings, but for His faithfulness behind the scenes. Choosing gratitude, especially when life feels heavy, is a sacrifice of praise. And over time, I've seen how that choice draws me closer to the heart of God.

Simple Ways to Live Out Sacrificial Worship

1. **Create Daily Worship Moments**

   Start each day by dedicating your time to God, even in small ways. This could be a prayer as you sip your coffee, reading a verse before heading to work, or listening to worship music during your commute.

2. **Speak Words of Life**

   How you interact with those around you—your spouse, children, coworkers—can be an act of worship. Choose to speak words of encouragement, love, and faith, even when it's difficult.

3. **Surrender Your Fears**

   When worry creeps in, turn it into a prayer. Release your anxieties to God and trust Him to carry them. This act of surrender is a profound form of worship.

4. **Express Gratitude**

   Whether it's through a journal, a prayer, or simply pausing to reflect, make gratitude a daily habit. Thank God for both the big blessings and the small mercies that often go unnoticed.

5. Serve Others

Acts of kindness and service, especially when they require time, effort, or resources, are powerful ways to worship. Look for opportunities to meet someone's need, whether it's through encouragement, practical help, or generosity.

Sacrificial worship isn't about perfection—it's about showing up with a willing heart, even when it's hard. Whether it's guiding your family, expressing gratitude in trials, or surrendering your fears, these acts of worship draw us closer to God and remind us of His unwavering presence. Let each moment of your life become an offering of praise to the One who is always faithful.

Chapter 11: **Worship as Intersession**

*"For my house will be called a house of prayer
for all nations."*

—ISAIAH 56:7

WORSHIP IS OFTEN SEEN as a deeply personal act, a time when we come before God to honor Him, express gratitude, and align our hearts with His will. While this personal aspect of worship is vital, there is a deeper dimension that often goes unnoticed—worship as intercession. This is worship that transcends the individual, becoming a bridge between heaven and earth for the sake of others. It is worship that carries the burdens of the world, brings God's presence into the broken places, and invites His will to be done on earth as it is in heaven.

In Isaiah 56:7, God declares, "For my house will be called a house of prayer for all nations." This verse reveals the global and intercessory nature of worship that God desires. His vision is for a people who not only seek Him for their own needs but also intercede for others and for the redemption of the nations. Worship, then, becomes more than an individual act of devotion—it becomes a communal and missional expression of God's heart.

Through prayerful songs, declarations of praise, and hearts fully surrendered to God, we can stand in the gap for others, bringing their needs and the world's crises before the throne of grace. This kind of worship calls us to move beyond ourselves, engaging in a form of praise that aligns with God's kingdom purposes. It challenges us to see worship not just as something we do for our own edification but as a powerful act of love, mercy, and spiritual warfare.

It is time to uncover the biblical foundation for intercessory worship, practical ways to engage in it, and the incredible impact it can have on individuals, communities, and the world. Let us open our hearts to the call of God to become intercessors in worship, joining Him in His mission to bring healing, hope, and salvation to the world.

The Biblical Foundation of Intercessory Worship

Isaiah 56:7 offers a profound insight into God's vision for worship: This declaration reveals God's inclusive heart and His desire for worship to serve as a vehicle for intercession. Worship in God's house is not limited to personal devotion; it is a communal, global act where believers lift up the needs of others and align their hearts with God's redemptive purposes.

As a worship leader, this verse became a guiding principle in how I approached every moment of praise. As we sang hymns like "It Is Well with My Soul," I was struck by the weight of the lyrics—not just as poetic expressions, but as declarations of faith. In those sacred moments, I could sense the presence of God moving through the room. Worship became more than just music; it became a spiritual weapon, a shield against despair, and a proclamation of hope in the hands of a praying church. The words "whatever my lot, Thou hast taught me to say, it is well . . . " were more than a melody—they were a battle cry for hearts choosing to trust God in the storm.

Scripture is filled with examples of intercessory worship. In Genesis, Abraham pleaded with God to spare Sodom and Gomorrah. This was not merely a conversation—it was an act of worshipful intercession. Abraham approached God with reverence, appealing to His justice and mercy on behalf of others.

In Exodus, Moses interceded for the Israelites after they sinned by worshiping the golden calf. As Moses stood in God's presence, he pleaded for mercy, reminding God of His promises. This was a profound act of worship, acknowledging God's greatness while interceding for a rebellious people.

The early church in Acts also modeled intercessory worship. When Peter was imprisoned, the believers gathered to pray fervently. Their worshipful intercession led to Peter's miraculous release, demonstrating the power of collective prayer and praise.

These stories remind us that intercessory worship is deeply rooted in Scripture. It calls us to move beyond self-focused praise and join God in His mission to heal and restore the world.

Worship as a Platform for Intercession

Worship provides a sacred platform for intercession, where the boundaries between heaven and earth blur, and God's presence becomes tangible. Through praise, prayer, and corporate worship, believers create a space for God to move powerfully in the lives of others.

Praise serves as one of the most profound forms of intercession. When we declare God's character and promises over situations, we invite His power to work. Psalm 22:3 says that God inhabits the praises of His people. This means that when we worship, we create an atmosphere where His presence can bring healing, peace, and transformation.

I've seen this truth come alive during worship services. On one occasion, during an eight month deployment, many were struggling with stress and separation from their families. As we sang songs like "It Is Well," I felt the Spirit moving, breaking down barriers and lifting burdens. One sailor later told me that the worship service gave him the strength to get through the deployment. Praise is not just an expression of faith—it's a conduit for God's intervention.

Prayer is another key aspect of intercessory worship. Worship songs often serve as prayers set to music, expressing hope, healing, and victory. When I planned worship, I often chose songs that reflected the needs of the congregation. Whether it was a hymn of comfort for those grieving or a song of victory for those facing battles, these musical prayers became powerful tools for intercession.

Corporate worship amplifies the impact of intercession. When believers gather to worship and pray, their collective faith can create a ripple effect that transforms lives. Jesus said, "For where two or three gather in my name, there am I with them" (Matthew 18:20).

Practical Ways to Engage in Intercessory Worship

Intercessory worship is not limited to special events; it can become a regular part of daily life. Personal worship provides an intimate space to pray for others while drawing closer to God. During my time in the Navy, I often used personal worship as a time to intercede for my family back home. Singing songs like "Blessed Assurance" while thinking of my wife and sons helped me feel connected to them and lifted their needs to God.

Corporate worship offers unique opportunities to engage in intercession. Sunday services can include prayers for global and local needs, helping congregations focus their worship on God's mission. I once led a service where we dedicated a portion of the time to praying for missionaries abroad. As we sang "Here I Am to Worship," the congregation prayed for boldness and protection for those serving in dangerous areas. It was a powerful reminder that worship can extend beyond the sanctuary to touch lives across the globe.

Creative expressions of worship can also serve as powerful acts of intercession. When we write songs, compose poetry, or craft heartfelt prayers that cry out for justice, healing, or mercy, we are not only expressing our own longings—we are standing in the gap for others. These artistic offerings become a voice for the voiceless, a lament for the hurting, and a call to action for the church.

Throughout history, many of the most enduring hymns and spiritual songs were born out of deep personal or communal struggle—moments where individuals turned their pain, conviction, or hope into a cry to God. These creative expressions often carry prophetic weight. They name what is broken, proclaim God's truth over it, and invite others to respond—not just with emotion, but with prayer, repentance, and renewed purpose.

When a songwriter pens a chorus asking God to "break our hearts for what breaks Yours," that line becomes more than just lyrics—it becomes a prayer of intercession that, when sung in unity, joins believers together in a shared burden for the world. When someone writes a poem that pours out grief over injustice or writes a prayer pleading for peace, they're inviting the Spirit to move not only in their own heart but in the hearts of all who engage with their words.

Creative worship doesn't just stir emotion—it awakens intercession. It reminds us that worship is not isolated from the suffering of the world but is deeply connected to it. It compels us to pray, to act, and to believe that God's kingdom will come on earth as it is in heaven.

The Impact of Intercessory Worship

Intercessory worship transforms individuals, communities, and the world. On a personal level, it deepens compassion and spiritual maturity. When I intercede through worship, I find my heart aligning with God's purposes, making me more aware of the needs around me.

On a communal level, intercessory worship releases God's power into specific situations. I've seen breakthroughs in families, churches, and communities during times of united worship and prayer. One church I attended had a worship service focused on intercession for local schools led to an outpouring of resources and support for underprivileged students.

On a global level, intercessory worship aligns with God's mission to reconcile the world to Himself. It reflects the church's role as a "house of prayer for all nations," embodying God's heart for humanity.

Incorporating intercessory worship into daily life begins with a commitment to pray for others while worshipping. Sensitivity to the Holy Spirit's leading can guide us to specific needs and situations. The church is uniquely positioned to foster a culture of intercessory worship, uniting believers in prayer and praise to make a global impact.

Worship is not just a personal act of devotion; it is a powerful form of intercession that brings God's presence into the lives of others. Through worship, we align our hearts with God's purposes and invite His will to be done on earth. As we embrace this calling, we become partners in His mission to redeem and restore the world.

Let us commit to lifting others in prayer and praise, trusting in God's power to move in miraculous ways. May our worship become a bridge that connects heaven and earth, bringing hope, healing, and transformation to all who encounter it.

Chapter 12: The Eternal Worship of Heaven

"Day and night they never stop saying: 'Holy, holy, holy is the Lord God Almighty, who was, and is, and is to come.'"

—REVELATION 4:8

THERE ARE MOMENTS IN life when the veil between heaven and earth feels incredibly thin. These moments, though rare, leave a lasting mark on the soul.

I remember standing alone on the deck of the ship one night, far out at sea. The sky was a blanket of stars, unpolluted and infinite, stretching from one horizon to the other. The only sounds were the steady pulse of the ocean and the low hum of the ship's engines beneath my boots. No voices, no instruments—just the deep silence of creation holding its breath.

And then, almost without thinking, I began to sing—"How Great Thou Art." It wasn't loud or polished, but it was honest. As the words left my mouth, I realized the sea, the stars, and the solitude had all become part of the chorus. In that moment, the vastness around me didn't feel empty; it felt full. As if heaven itself had leaned a little closer.

That night has never left me. Not because there was anything grand or staged about it—but because it was a glimpse of something greater, something eternal. A whisper of the worship that surrounds the throne of God, described in Revelation 4. Out there, under the canopy of heaven and the rhythm of the deep, I understood worship not just as song, but as surrender.

Our journey concludes—both in spirit and in destination—at the throne room of heaven, as revealed to the apostle John. This breathtaking vision is more than a prophecy of what is to come; it is an invitation to reimagine how we worship in the here and now. The heavenly worship described in Revelation isn't distant or detached—it beckons us to draw near with reverence, awe, and expectancy. It reminds us that our earthly worship is a rehearsal for eternity, a sacred preparation for the day when we will join the everlasting chorus surrounding the throne of God.

The Vision of Heavenly Worship

When John received the vision of heaven recorded in Revelation 4, he was in exile on the island of Patmos. His earthly circumstances were bleak—isolated, persecuted, and seemingly defeated. Cut off from the familiar comforts of community and worship, John faced what many would see as a hopeless situation. Yet, in the midst of his isolation, God chose to reveal a vision so profound that it transcended his physical and emotional limitations. This revelation not only lifted John's spirit but also offered a glimpse of eternal realities that would inspire generations of believers.

The vision begins with a door standing open in heaven. This is no ordinary doorway—it is an invitation into the very presence of God. A voice, like the sound of a trumpet, calls out to John, "Come up here." The language is commanding yet welcoming, emphasizing the divine authority of the one who speaks. This moment sets the tone for the entire chapter: God is drawing John (and by extension, all of us) into a reality far greater than the struggles and trials of this earthly life.

What John saw when he stepped through that open door was extraordinary. At the center of it all was a throne, not just any throne, but *the throne*—the focal point of all heaven and earth. The throne was surrounded by brilliance and majesty beyond human comprehension. John uses descriptive language, speaking of flashes of lightning, rumblings of thunder, and a sea of glass like crystal, yet even these images can only approximate the reality of what he witnessed. The throne was not just a symbol of authority; it was a declaration of God's sovereignty over all creation. In a world where rulers and kingdoms rise and fall, this throne stands eternal, a reminder that no power on earth can rival the power of God.

Surrounding the throne were four living creatures, each unique in form and covered with eyes all around, even under their wings. These beings are unlike anything in our natural world, representing the fullness of God's creation—strength, intelligence, swiftness, and nobility. Their eyes symbolize divine perception and insight, seeing all things. Day and night, without pause, they cry out, "Holy, holy, holy is the Lord God Almighty, who was, and is, and is to come." Their praise is a declaration of God's eternal nature and unchanging holiness. The repetition of "holy" three times emphasizes the infinite depth of God's purity and separateness from sin.

This ceaseless declaration of God's holiness creates a rhythm in heaven that echoes throughout eternity. It is not born out of obligation but from a place of awe and truth. These creatures are so overwhelmed by the greatness of God that their worship flows naturally and unceasingly. In their example, we see that true worship is not something that can be contained or scheduled; it is an ongoing response to the revelation of who God is.

But the vision doesn't stop there. Surrounding the throne are twenty-four elders, seated on their own thrones yet continually deferring to the central throne of God. These elders, often interpreted as representatives of the twelve tribes of Israel and the twelve apostles, symbolize the completeness of God's redeemed people. Clothed in white robes and wearing crowns of gold, they signify victory and purity—gifts from the One they worship. Yet, in the presence of God, even these symbols of honor are cast down before His throne. As they fall prostrate, they proclaim, "You are worthy, our Lord and God, to receive glory and honor and power, for you created all things, and by your will they were created and have their being."

This act of casting their crowns is profoundly significant. The crowns, representative of achievements, authority, and rewards, are not kept as personal trophies but are offered back to God. In this gesture, the elders acknowledge that everything they have comes from Him and that He alone is worthy of all glory. Their worship is not about what they have achieved but about exalting the One who enabled it all.

For those of us reading this vision today, it's easy to feel disconnected from such a transcendent scene. The imagery is otherworldly, the creatures unimaginable, and the sheer majesty overwhelming. Yet, as we take a closer look, we begin to see how this heavenly worship is not so distant after all. The themes of reverence, awe, and unceasing praise provide a model for how we are to worship here and now.

Reverence is foundational to worship. The living creatures and elders approach the throne with deep respect, fully aware of God's holiness. In a world where casualness often seeps into our view of worship, this vision reminds us that God deserves our utmost honor. Awe flows naturally from this reverence. The elders and living creatures are not compelled to worship out of duty but are driven by the overwhelming greatness of God. Their awe fuels their worship, reminding us that true worship is not about fulfilling a ritual but about responding to the majesty of the Creator.

Unceasing praise challenges us to rethink the boundaries we place on worship. The living creatures declare God's holiness day and night, a stark contrast to the way we often compartmentalize worship into specific times and places. This is not to say that we are called to sing non-stop, but rather to adopt a posture of continual worship—a life lived in gratitude, acknowledgment, and surrender to God's glory.

As we read Revelation 4, we are not just spectators of a heavenly scene. We are invited into its rhythms and meaning. The worship of heaven is not a distant reality reserved for a future time; it is a present call to align our hearts with the eternal truths it reveals. In every prayer, every song, every moment of silence, we echo the cries of "Holy, holy, holy," joining the heavenly chorus in proclaiming God's worthiness.

This vision transforms our understanding of worship, inviting us to move beyond the superficial and embrace a deeper, more reverent approach to the throne of God. Through John's experience, we are reminded that no matter our circumstances—whether in exile like him, or in the busyness of our daily lives—God's majesty transcends our limitations and invites us into eternal worship.

Reverence and Awe: The Foundation of Worship

One of the most striking aspects of heavenly worship is the overwhelming sense of reverence. The creatures and elders in Revelation 4 are consumed by the holiness of God. Their worship is not casual or routine; it is an all-encompassing response to who God is.

This reverence is something we often struggle to replicate on earth. In a culture that prioritizes convenience and entertainment, it's easy for worship to become just another item on the weekly checklist. I've noticed this tendency in my own life, especially during busy seasons. As a worship leader, there were times when leading worship felt more like a duty than a privilege. But every time I opened my Bible to passages like Revelation 4, I was reminded of the holiness of God and the weight of what it means to worship Him.

Holiness, as revealed in this vision, is not just an attribute of God—it is the essence of His being. The cry of "Holy, holy, holy" is not a mere repetition for emphasis; it is an acknowledgment of God's complete otherness. He is set apart, pure, and perfect. In the presence of such holiness, the only appropriate response is worship.

Unceasing Praise: Worship as a Lifestyle

The worship described in Revelation is not confined to a particular time or place. The living creatures praise God day and night, without ceasing. This unending worship challenges our earthly perspective, where worship is often limited to Sunday mornings or specific gatherings.

For years, I struggled to see worship as more than an event. It wasn't until I experienced extended deployments at sea that I began to understand the concept of worship as a lifestyle. There were no traditional church services or choirs on those long voyages, yet worship found its way into my daily routine. Whether it was through silent prayers during morning watch or singing hymns with a handful of sailors, worship became an integral part of my life.

Unceasing praise is not about singing nonstop; it's about living in a constant state of gratitude and awareness of God's presence. The living creatures' unending declaration of God's holiness serves as a reminder that worship is not just something we do—it's who we are as believers.

Casting Our Crowns: A Lesson in Surrender

The twenty-four elders casting their crowns before God's throne is one of the most powerful images in Revelation 4. Crowns, symbolizing authority and achievement, are laid at the feet of the One who is truly worthy. This act of surrender reflects the heart of worship.

For me, this imagery has always been deeply personal. As a Navy Chief, my uniform and rank represented years of hard work and dedication. Yet, when I became a Christian, I realized that even my greatest achievements were gifts from God. The elders' example challenges us to lay down our accomplishments, our pride, and even our struggles, recognizing that everything we have comes from Him.

There have been moments in my life when I felt the weight of responsibility and the temptation to rely on my own strength.

But Revelation 4 reminds me that true worship begins with surrender. It's about acknowledging that God is the source of all we have and all we are.

Transforming Earthly Worship

The vision of heavenly worship is not just a glimpse of the future; it is a call to action for the present. When we align our worship with the pattern set in Revelation, we begin to experience a deeper connection with God.

One way we can transform our worship is by making God the center of everything. Too often, we approach worship with a consumer mindset, focusing on what we can get out of it rather than what we can offer to God. But Revelation challenges us to shift our focus. Worship is not about our preferences; it's about God's worthiness.

Another lesson we can learn from heavenly worship is the importance of unity. In Revelation 4, all of heaven joins together in glorifying God. This unity stands in stark contrast to the divisions that often plague earthly churches. When we come together with one heart and one purpose, our worship becomes a powerful witness to the world.

Finally, the vision of heaven reminds us that worship is preparation for eternity. Every time we gather to sing, pray, or serve, we are rehearsing for the day when we will stand before God's throne. This perspective changes how we approach worship, filling it with anticipation and joy.

Living for the Throne

As I reflect on the worship service aboard the ship, I realize that what made it special was not the setting or the music—it was the focus on God. For a moment, we were caught up in something bigger than ourselves, a foretaste of the eternal worship described in Revelation.

Revelation 4 calls us to worship with that same reverence, awe, and anticipation. It invites us to cast our crowns, lift our voices, and live our lives in a way that honors God. Let us join the heavenly chorus, declaring, "Holy, holy, holy is the Lord God Almighty, who was, and is, and is to come."

A Deeper Look: **Study Guide**

Chapter One: The Essence of Worship

1. Deeper in Scripture

In this section, we will examine key passages that reveal the heart of worship and what it means to worship in spirit and in truth. Each verse will offer insights into how we can align our worship with God's Word.

- John 4:23:

  "Yet a time is coming and has now come when the true worshipers will worship the Father in the Spirit and in truth, for they are the kind of worshipers the Father seeks."

  - Questions for reflection: What does it mean to worship in spirit and in truth? How does this passage challenge your current understanding of worship?

  - Application: Identify areas in your life where worship has been more about outward actions rather than a heartfelt response to God. How can you shift toward worship that is more in spirit and truth?

- Romans 12:1:

  "Therefore, I urge you, brothers and sisters, in view of God's mercy, to offer your bodies as a living sacrifice, holy and pleasing to God—this is your true and proper worship."

- Questions for reflection: How does offering your body as a living sacrifice represent true worship? What does this look like in your daily life?

- Application: Consider how your everyday actions—work, family interactions, hobbies—can be offered as acts of worship to God. How can you make your life a living sacrifice?

- Psalm 29:2:

  "Ascribe to the LORD the glory due his name; worship the LORD in the splendor of his holiness."

  - Questions for reflection: What does it mean to give God the glory due His name? How can you worship Him in the splendor of His holiness?

  - Application: Spend time meditating on God's holiness. How does understanding His character transform the way you approach worship?

2. Reflection on Chapter Material

In this section, we will reflect on key points from the chapter to deepen our understanding of what true worship looks like in daily life.

- **Worship as a Heart Posture**

  Worship is more than an outward expression; it's a heart response to God. How does this change the way you view traditional forms of worship (such as singing, praying, and attending church services)?

  - Reflect on times in your life when worship was more about routine or habit than about a genuine connection with God. What shifted your focus during those times?

- In what ways can you begin to cultivate a heart of worship that isn't dependent on circumstances or physical locations?

• What Worship Is Not

Worship is not limited to singing or something that only happens within a church service. How does knowing this open up opportunities to worship God in every aspect of life?

- Reflect on how you've previously viewed worship. Have you ever felt limited in your expression of worship? How can you begin to expand your understanding of worship beyond traditional forms?

- Consider how you might turn everyday tasks (work, spending time with family, personal hobbies) into acts of worship by offering them to God.

• Worship as a Relationship

Worship is part of our ongoing relationship with God. How does this relational aspect influence the way you approach worship?

- Reflect on the comparison between worship and communication in a relationship. How does this analogy challenge you to pursue deeper, more intimate worship with God?

- Think of a relationship in your life that thrives because of consistent communication and intentionality. How can you apply that same consistency and intentionality to your worship of God?

3. Journal Prompts

Take time to journal your thoughts and prayers as you work through this study guide. Let the following prompts guide your reflections:

- Heart of Worship:

  "What does it mean for me to worship God in spirit and in truth? How is my heart aligned with God's desire for authentic worship, and where do I need to grow?"

  - Write down your personal definition of true worship, based on what you've learned in this chapter. Ask God to reveal areas of your life where you may be going through the motions rather than worshiping from the heart.

- Worship Beyond Sunday:

  "In what ways can I make worship a daily practice, not just something that happens on Sunday?"

  - Make a list of the different areas of your life where you can incorporate worship—at home, at work, during daily routines. Write down one specific action you can take each day to intentionally worship God in those spaces. [/BL 1]

- Worship in Difficult Times:

  "How can I worship God in the midst of challenges or difficult circumstances?"

  - Reflect on a time when life's circumstances made it hard to worship. Write about how you can continue to worship God even when things aren't going as planned. Offer a prayer, asking God to help you focus on His goodness and faithfulness in every season.

By walking through these sections, you can deepen your understanding of what true worship is, reflect on how this applies to your life, and take meaningful steps toward making worship a central part of your daily relationship with God.

Chapter Two: Worship is a Lifestyle

Section 1: Deeper in Scripture

The chapter explores several passages that form the biblical foundation for living a life of worship. In this section, you'll focus on studying these key scriptures.

Romans 12:1-2

- Key Verse: "Therefore, I urge you, brothers and sisters, in view of God's mercy, to offer your bodies as a living sacrifice, holy and pleasing to God—this is your true and proper worship. Do not conform to the pattern of this world, but be transformed by the renewing of your mind. Then you will be able to test and approve what God's will is—his good, pleasing and perfect will."

- Study Questions:

    – What does it mean to offer your body as a living sacrifice?

    – How does the renewing of the mind relate to worship?

    – In what ways can you discern God's will in your daily life?

Isaiah 29:13

- Key Verse: "These people come near to me with their mouth and honor me with their lips, but their hearts are far from me. Their worship of me is based on merely human rules they have been taught."

- Study Questions:

    – What is the danger of worshiping with the wrong heart?

    – How does this verse challenge your understanding of genuine worship?

Proverbs 3:5-6

- Key Verse: "Trust in the Lord with all your heart and lean not on your own understanding; in all your ways submit to him, and he will make your paths straight."
- Study Questions:
  - How does trusting God impact the decisions you make?
  - What does it look like to submit your plans and decisions to God in everyday life?

Section 2: Reflection on the Chapter Material

In this section, reflect on the key themes of the chapter as they apply to your own life. Consider the following reflection questions:

1. **Actions as Worship**

   - Think of a time when your actions reflected or contradicted your faith. How did your actions affect your witness to others?
   - Are there areas in your life where your actions are inconsistent with your worship of God? How can you bring those areas in line with a life of worship?

2. **Attitude as Worship**

   - Reflect on the attitudes you bring into your daily life. Are there any negative attitudes (e.g., pride, bitterness, self-reliance) that hinder your worship? How can you adopt an attitude of humility and submission to God's will?

- How do you approach God in worship? Is your heart fully engaged, or do you find yourself going through the motions?

3. Decisions as Worship

- Think about a recent decision you made. Did you seek God's guidance before making that decision? How did that decision reflect your trust in God?

- How can you bring more of your decision-making process into alignment with God's will, as an act of worship?

Section 3: Journal Prompt

Use the following prompts to guide your personal reflection and journaling:

1. Actions:

- Write about an area in your life where you feel your actions are not aligning with your faith. What specific steps can you take to bring your actions into harmony with your desire to worship God?

2. Attitude:

- Reflect on your current attitude toward God. Are there any negative attitudes you need to address? Write about how you can shift your perspective to adopt an attitude of worship and gratitude in your daily life.

3. Decisions:

- Think of an important decision you are facing right now. Journal about how you can approach this decision with a heart of worship, seeking God's will above your own.

What steps can you take to make this decision a reflection of your dependence on God?

This study guide is designed to help you grow deeper in your understanding of worship as a lifestyle. Through scripture study, reflection, and journaling, may you experience a deeper connection to God and live out your faith in a way that honors Him in every aspect of your life.

Chapter Three: Worship as a Weapon

Section 1: Deeper in Scripture

In this section, we'll dive deeper into the key biblical passages that form the foundation of this chapter. Use these questions and reflections to enhance your understanding of worship as a spiritual weapon.

1. 2 Chronicles 20:21-22 (NIV)

    "After consulting the people, Jehoshaphat appointed men to sing to the Lord and to praise him for the splendor of his holiness as they went out at the head of the army, saying: 'Give thanks to the Lord, for his love endures forever.'"

    – What does this passage reveal about Jehoshaphat's faith in God?

    – Why do you think Jehoshaphat sent worshipers ahead of the army rather than soldiers?

    – How does this act of faith demonstrate the power of worship in spiritual battles?

2. Ephesians 6:12 (NIV)

    "For our struggle is not against flesh and blood, but against the rulers, against the authorities, against the powers of this dark

world and against the spiritual forces of evil in the heavenly realms."

- How does this verse explain the nature of our spiritual battles?

- What role can worship play in standing firm against the spiritual forces mentioned in this verse?

- How can we apply this understanding of spiritual warfare in our daily lives?

3. Psalm 22:3 (NIV)

   "Yet you are enthroned as the Holy One; you are the one Israel praises."

   - What does it mean that God "inhabits" the praises of His people?

   - How does worship invite God's presence into our situations?

   - In what ways have you experienced God's presence during times of worship?

4. Psalm 8:2 (NIV)

   "Through the praise of children and infants you have established a stronghold against your enemies, to silence the foe and the avenger."

   - What does this verse suggest about the power of worship in spiritual warfare?

   - How does worship silence the enemy in your life?

Section 2: Reflection on the Chapter Material

In this section, take time to reflect on key themes and insights from the chapter, focusing on how worship can serve as a spiritual weapon in your own life.

1. **Worship as a Declaration of Faith**

   In the chapter, we saw how Jehoshaphat's decision to send worshipers ahead of the army was an act of profound faith. Reflect on moments in your life when you've had to trust God in the face of overwhelming circumstances.

   – How did your faith grow in those moments?
   – How can worship help you strengthen your faith when facing spiritual battles?

2. **The Atmosphere of Worship**

   Worship has the power to shift spiritual atmospheres and invite God's presence. Reflect on a time when worship changed your perspective or brought peace in a difficult situation.

   – How did worship impact your emotions, thoughts, or circumstances?
   – What changes do you notice in your heart and mind when you engage in genuine worship?

3. **Worship as a Form of Surrender**

   Worship is a posture of surrender, acknowledging that God is in control. Reflect on areas of your life where you are holding on to control or struggling to surrender to God.

   – What would it look like to surrender these areas to God through worship?
   – How can you practice daily surrender through worship, even in small moments?

4. Victory Through Worship

The story of Jehoshaphat shows us that victory can be won through worship, even when it seems like we are outnumbered or outmatched. Reflect on battles you are currently facing, whether spiritual, emotional, or relational.

   - How can you incorporate worship into your battle plan?
   - What might it look like to worship God in the midst of this struggle, trusting Him for victory?

5. Personal Testimony of Worship

In the chapter, I shared some personal reflections on how worship has been a weapon in my own battles. Take time to reflect on your own testimony of worship.

   - When has worship brought you closer to God in difficult seasons?
   - What victories have you experienced as a result of worship?

Section 3: Journal Prompts

Use these prompts to guide personal journaling time as you process the lessons from this chapter and seek to apply them in your life.

1. Worship as a Weapon

Write about a time when worship helped you through a difficult situation or spiritual battle. What role did worship play in bringing peace, clarity, or victory?

   - How did that experience deepen your understanding of God's power in your life?

2. Facing the Enemy with Worship

Consider the battles you are currently facing. How can you approach these struggles through worship? What specific worship practices can you incorporate into your life to invite God's presence and power into these situations?

– Write out a prayer or praise that you can offer to God in the midst of this battle.

3. The Atmosphere of Worship

Think about how worship changes the atmosphere—both in your heart and in the world around you. Reflect on the moments when worship shifted your perspective or filled you with peace.

– How can you intentionally cultivate a heart of worship in your daily life, even outside of corporate worship services?

4. Worship as Surrender

Write about an area of your life where you are struggling to surrender control to God. How might worship help you release this area into God's hands? What would it look like to worship God as an act of surrender in this situation?

– Journal about any fears, doubts, or desires you have around this area, and how you can use worship to bring them before God.

5. Victory Through Worship

Reflect on a current challenge or spiritual battle you are facing. How can you "raise a hallelujah" in the midst of this situation? What specific steps can you take to worship your way through this battle?

- Journal a prayer or declaration of faith that you can speak over your situation as an act of worship and trust in God's victory.

Conclusion

By engaging in Scripture, reflecting on the chapter's themes, and journaling your thoughts and prayers, you will deepen your understanding of how worship can serve as a powerful weapon in spiritual warfare. Remember, worship isn't just something we do in response to victory—it's often the very thing that leads us to victory. Embrace worship as an essential tool in your daily battles, trusting that God will fight for you as you lift your praise to Him.

Chapter Four: Worship In Humility

Section 1: Deeper in Scripture

Use the following passages to deepen your understanding of the relationship between humility and worship. Read each passage carefully and consider how it connects to the themes of the chapter.

1. Micah 6:8—"He has shown you, O mortal, what is good. And what does the Lord require of you? To act justly, to love mercy, and to walk humbly with your God."

   - How does this verse define what God requires of us? What does it mean to "walk humbly" with God in your daily life?
   - Consider how humility impacts your relationship with God and others.

2. John 4:23—"Yet a time is coming and has now come when the true worshipers will worship the Father in the Spirit and in truth, for they are the kind of worshipers the Father seeks."

- Reflect on what it means to worship in spirit and truth. How does humility play a role in becoming the kind of worshiper God seeks?

3. Philippians 2:5-8—"Let this attitude be in you, which was also in Christ Jesus. . . He humbled Himself by becoming obedient to death—even death on a cross."

   - What does Paul's description of Christ's humility teach us about the nature of true worship and surrender?

   - How does Christ's example of humility challenge you in your approach to worship and everyday life?

4. Mark 10:17-22—The story of the Rich Young Ruler.

   - What was the rich young ruler's stumbling block when it came to humility and surrender? How does this relate to the obstacles you might face in fully surrendering to God?

   - What can you learn from the ruler's decision, and how might his story prompt a deeper surrender in your own life?

5. John 13:12-15—Jesus washing the feet of His disciples.

   - How does Jesus' act of service illustrate humility in worship?

   - Consider what foot-washing might look like in your own context. How can you serve others as an act of worship?

Section 2: Reflection on the Chapter Material

Take some time to reflect on the key themes and ideas from the chapter. Use the questions below to guide your reflection.

1. Humility in Worship

   – How does humility shape our worship experience? Why
     is it essential to approach God with a humble heart?

   – Reflect on the statement: "Worshiping God in humility
     isn't about impressing Him with our deeds or possessions;
     it is about approaching Him with a heart of submission."
     How does this change your understanding of worship?

2. The Battle Between Humility and Vanity

   – Think about the internal battle between humility and
     vanity. How does vanity or pride manifest in your own
     life, and how might it interfere with your worship of God?

   – The Rich Young Ruler's struggle was with wealth, but
     what might be the "riches" in your life that keep you from
     fully surrendering to God?

3. Surrendering Daily to God

   – The chapter describes humility as a daily act of surrender.
     What does this daily surrender look like for you? How
     can you more intentionally surrender your will to God
     each day?

   – Jesus' example of humility calls us to follow in His foot-
     steps. How can you practically live out humility in your
     relationships, your work, and your worship?

4. Christ as the Ultimate Example of Humility

   – How does Christ's willingness to humble Himself—de-
     spite His divinity—impact your understanding of wor-
     ship and service? How does His example of washing the
     disciples' feet challenge you to rethink your own approach
     to serving others?

   – What are some ways that you can embody Christ's humil-
     ity in your life today?

5. Walking Humbly with God

   - In what ways can you "walk humbly" with God in your personal worship, relationships, and daily actions? Reflect on practical steps you can take to live out the teachings of Micah 6:8.

Section 3: Journal Prompts

Use the following journal prompts to reflect personally and explore your thoughts about humility and worship.

1. The Battle Between Pride and Humility

   - What are some areas in your life where you struggle with pride or vanity? How does this affect your relationship with God and others?

   - Write about a time when you felt challenged to surrender something to God. How did you respond, and what was the outcome?

2. Surrendering Your Will to God

   - What are you holding onto that prevents you from fully surrendering to God in humility? Is it control over your future, fear of the unknown, or attachment to comfort or security? How can you take a step toward surrendering that area of your life to God?

   - Write a prayer asking God to help you release what stands in the way of your worship and dependence on Him.

3. Christ's Example of Humility

   - Reflect on how Christ's humility influences your understanding of true worship. How does His willingness to serve impact the way you approach serving others in your own life?

- Write about a practical way you can follow Christ's example of humility this week, whether in your family, church, or workplace.

4. Daily Acts of Humility

- What does daily humility look like in your life? How can you practice humility in your words, actions, and decisions?

- Reflect on a recent experience where you either succeeded or failed to act humbly. What did you learn from that experience, and how can it guide your future actions?

5. Walking Humbly with God

- What does it mean for you to "walk humbly with your God"? Write about how you can incorporate this mindset into your daily routine, your prayers, and your worship.

- Identify one specific way you can walk humbly with God this week. Write a commitment to God and yourself to take that step, and reflect on how you will follow through.

Final Thoughts

Humility is central to the worship journey, and it is a posture that we are called to embrace in every area of life. As you study these scriptures, reflect on the chapter material, and engage in the journaling prompts, seek to align your heart more closely with the humility of Christ. Surrendering your will to God daily is the essence of true worship, and it is through this humility that we can walk more faithfully with our Lord.

Chapter Five: Worship and Obedience

Section 1: Deeper in Scripture

In this section, we will dive deeper into the key scriptures from the chapter to better understand the importance of obedience as the highest form of worship. Use these questions and reflections to guide your study:

1 Samuel 15:22-23 (NIV)

"Does the Lord delight in burnt offerings and sacrifices as much as in obeying the Lord? To obey is better than sacrifice, and to heed is better than the fat of rams. For rebellion is like the sin of divination, and arrogance like the evil of idolatry. Because you have rejected the word of the Lord, he has rejected you as king."

- Why does Samuel emphasize that obedience is better than sacrifice?

- Reflect on the historical and spiritual context. Why was Saul's partial obedience a problem, and how does that relate to our modern-day choices when it comes to following God's instructions?

- Consider what this scripture teaches about the nature of true worship and the weight of obedience over religious rituals.

John 14:15 (NIV)

"If you love me, keep my commands."

- What does Jesus mean by this statement?

- How does love for Christ naturally lead to obedience, and how does that obedience reflect our worship?

- How does this connect with the message from Samuel to Saul? Are there areas in your life where obedience feels challenging, and how might that be hindering your worship?

Deuteronomy 10:12-13 (NIV)

"And now, Israel, what does the LORD your God ask of you but to fear the LORD your God, to walk in obedience to him, to love him, to serve the LORD your God with all your heart and with all your soul, and to observe the LORD's commands and decrees that I am giving you today for your own good?"

- Why is obedience described as "for your own good"?
- Reflect on the practical and spiritual benefits of walking in obedience to God's commands. How does obedience safeguard us, guide us, and ultimately bring us closer to God's heart?

Additional Scriptures for Further Study

- Romans 12:1-2 — Living sacrifice as worship.
- Isaiah 55:9 — God's thoughts are higher than ours, requiring trust and obedience.
- Acts 5:29 — "We must obey God rather than men."

Section 2: Reflection on the Chapter Material

In this section, reflect on the key themes and lessons from the chapter, and think about how they apply to your life and faith journey.

1. **Obedience Over Sacrifice**

   Reflect on the story of King Saul and Samuel's rebuke. How often do we, like Saul, offer sacrifices to God—whether in the form of religious duty, good works, or outward expressions of devotion—while neglecting what He truly asks of us: complete obedience?

– Reflection Question:

Are there areas in your life where you're offering "sacrifices" to God (e.g., religious activities, time, or resources) while avoiding full obedience in something specific He's asked of you?

2. The Cost of Disobedience

Saul's disobedience cost him his kingship and future blessings. Disobedience, even in seemingly small ways, can prevent us from experiencing the fullness of what God has planned for us.

– Reflection Question:

Are there areas in your life where you might be experiencing the consequences of disobedience? How might full obedience open up opportunities for God's blessings?

3. Obedience as Worship

Obedience is an act of love and worship to God. It shows trust in His sovereignty, a submission to His will, and a desire to honor Him above our own desires. True worship flows from a heart aligned with God's purposes through obedience.

– Reflection Question:

Do you view obedience as an act of worship in your own life? How might embracing this perspective transform the way you live out your faith?

Section 3: Journal Prompts

In this section, take time to journal your thoughts, prayers, and reflections in response to the chapter's themes. These prompts are designed to help you process what you've learned and apply it to your personal spiritual walk.

1. Reflect on a Time of Partial Obedience:

   Write about a time in your life when you obeyed God partially, like Saul, but held back in some way. What were your motivations? How did things turn out? What might you have done differently if you had trusted and fully obeyed God?

2. Surrendering in Obedience:

   Consider an area of your life where you know God is calling you to obedience, but you've been hesitant or resistant. Write a prayer of surrender, asking God for the courage and faith to fully obey His command. What steps can you take this week to move toward that obedience?

3. Worship Through Obedience:

   How does the idea of obedience as the highest form of worship resonate with you? Reflect on specific ways you can make obedience a central part of your worship, whether in your relationships, work, or personal spiritual disciplines. How can your daily decisions reflect a life of worship through obedience?

4. Listening to God's Voice:

   Journaling prompt: Reflect on how well you listen for God's voice in your daily life. Do you carve out time to hear from Him? How can you improve your attentiveness to His guidance through Scripture, prayer, and the Holy Spirit? Write about a time when you felt God speaking to you clearly and how you responded.

5. Praying for Strength in Obedience:

   Sometimes obedience is hard because it asks us to give up control, comfort, or convenience. Take a moment to write out a prayer, asking God to strengthen your heart for obedience. Ask for wisdom, discernment, and a deeper trust in His plans, even when they don't align with your expectations.

Closing Thoughts

As you work through these sections, remember that obedience is a lifelong journey of faith. God is not seeking perfection, but a willing heart that desires to honor Him in all things. Let your pursuit of obedience flow from a place of love and worship, knowing that as you obey, you are drawing closer to the heart of God. Use this guide to reflect, challenge yourself, and deepen your relationship with God through a life of obedience and worship.

Chapter 6: Worship in the Wilderness.

1. Deeper in Scripture

This section will help you dive into the scriptures referenced in the chapter and explore their significance in more depth.

- **Exodus 15:1-2 (NIV):**

  "I will sing to the Lord, for he is highly exalted. Both horse and driver he has hurled into the sea. The Lord is my strength and my defense; he has become my salvation. He is my God, and I will praise him, my father's God, and I will exalt him."

  - Context: After God miraculously delivered the Israelites from the pursuing Egyptians by parting the Red Sea, Moses and Miriam led the people in a song of praise. This passage captures the moment of worship that followed Israel's deliverance, showing how worship is a response to God's mighty works.

  - Reflection Question: In what ways has God delivered you from situations where you felt trapped or overwhelmed? How did you respond? Did worship play a role in that response?

- Exodus 14:11-12 (NLT):

  "They said to Moses, 'Was it because there were no graves in Egypt that you brought us to the desert to die? What have you done to us by bringing us out of Egypt? Didn't we say to you in Egypt, "Leave us alone; let us serve the Egyptians"? It would have been better for us to serve the Egyptians than to die in the desert!'"

  - Context: The Israelites, feeling trapped by the Red Sea on one side and the Egyptian army on the other, gave in to fear. Rather than turning to God in faith and worship, they expressed doubt and regret.

  - Reflection Question: When you face difficult situations, do you tend to react in fear or faith? How can you cultivate a heart of worship even in moments of anxiety and uncertainty?

- Psalm 62:6-7 (NLT):

  "He alone is my rock and my salvation, my fortress where I will not be shaken. My victory and honor come from God alone. He is my refuge, a rock where no enemy can reach me."

  - Context: David wrote these words during a time of hardship, yet his faith remained steadfast. His worship declared God's power and sovereignty, even before deliverance came.

  - Reflection Question: How does David's example of worship during hardship encourage you to trust in God's provision? What situations in your life could benefit from this type of unwavering trust?

2. Reflection on the Chapter Material

This section is designed to help you reflect on the chapter's main points and how they apply to your life.

- **Worship in Dark Times:**

  One of the central themes of this chapter is the importance of worship during our most difficult moments. When we are in the midst of suffering or spiritual dryness, worship can feel like the last thing we want to do, but it is often the most necessary. Worship draws us closer to God and reorients our hearts away from our problems and toward His power and goodness.

  - Reflection Question: Think about a time when you were going through a personal storm. How did you approach God during that time? Did you find it difficult to worship, or did worship help you draw closer to Him?

- **Fear vs. Faith in the Wilderness:**

  Just as the Israelites allowed fear to dominate their hearts when they were trapped by the Red Sea, we often let fear drown out our worship when life becomes overwhelming. But God calls us to worship even in the face of fear, as an act of trust and faith.

  - Reflection Question: What are some fears or obstacles in your life that have caused you to lose focus on God's sovereignty? How can you shift your perspective to worship in the midst of those fears?

- **The Power of Worship to Shift Our Focus:**

  Worship changes our focus. Instead of letting our problems consume us, worship helps us remember that God is greater than any challenge we face. It becomes an act of surrender, allowing God to take control while we rest in His promises.

  - Reflection Question: How has worship helped you shift your focus from your problems to God's sovereignty in the past? How might it help you in your current struggles?

3. Journal Prompts

Use these prompts to reflect on your personal experiences and thoughts as you apply the chapter's teachings to your life.

- Prompt 1:

  Think back to a time when you felt trapped by a difficult situation, much like the Israelites did when they were caught between the Red Sea and Pharaoh's army. How did you respond to that situation? Did you find yourself reacting in fear or turning to God in worship? Write about what you learned from that experience and how you might approach similar situations differently in the future.

- Prompt 2:

  Reflect on a season of spiritual dryness or hardship in your life. How did your relationship with God change during that time? Did you find it difficult to worship? What role, if any, did worship play in your healing and restoration? Write about how you can make worship a more central part of your life during challenging times.

- Prompt 3:

  David's declaration in Psalm 62 reminds us that God is our rock and salvation, even when we face difficulties. Write about a current challenge or storm in your life. How can you incorporate worship into your response to this situation, trusting that God is working for your good, even if you can't see the way forward yet?

This study guide is designed to help you dive deeper into the themes of *Worship in the Wilderness*, encouraging reflection on scripture, personal experience, and your journey of faith.

Chapter 7: Worshiping In All Seasons

Section 1: Deeper in Scripture

In this section, you will explore key Scriptures that align with the themes of worship, looking at David's example of worship in various seasons. Read and meditate on these passages to gain a deeper understanding of how David's relationship with God was defined by his worship.

Worship in Triumph

- 1 Chronicles 16:8-10: David's song of thanks after bringing the Ark of the Covenant to Jerusalem.
  - Reflection Question: How does David express gratitude in this passage? How can we cultivate a similar heart of thankfulness in moments of victory or success?

- 2 Samuel 6:14-16: David dances before the Lord as the Ark is brought into Jerusalem.
  - Reflection Question: What can we learn from David's unrestrained worship? How does his willingness to celebrate God challenge how we approach worship in joyful moments?

Worship in Lament

- Psalm 64:1-10: David's cry for deliverance from his enemies.
  - Reflection Question: In this Psalm, how does David balance his emotions of fear and trust? How does his lament lead him back to hope in God?

- Psalm 109:21-31: David's prayer for God's help in a time of betrayal and suffering.

- Reflection Question: How does David bring his pain before God while still acknowledging His sovereignty? How can lament be a form of worship in our own lives?

Worship in Repentance

- Psalm 51:1-12: David's prayer of repentance after his sin with Bathsheba.

  - Reflection Question: What is the significance of David asking for a "pure heart" and a "steadfast spirit"? How does this prayer teach us about the heart of repentance in worship?

- 2 Samuel 12:13-17: David's immediate response of repentance after Nathan confronts him.

  - Reflection Question: How does David's willingness to confess and seek forgiveness deepen our understanding of worship as more than celebration, but also humility before God?

Worship in Loss

- 2 Samuel 12:20-23: David's response of worship after the death of his child.

  - Reflection Question: How does David's worship in the face of loss show his trust in God? How can we worship in times of grief or unanswered prayers?

Section 2: Reflection on the Chapter Material

Take time to reflect on the themes of worship explored in the chapter. These questions and reflections are meant to help you connect with the material more deeply and think about how these truths can be applied in your own life.

1. **Worship in All Seasons**

   David's life exemplifies that worship is not tied to external circumstances but is a heart posture that remains focused on God in every season—whether in joy, sorrow, repentance, or loss.

   - Reflection: Think about your current season of life. Are you in a season of triumph, lament, repentance, or loss? How is your worship reflective of this season? How can you approach God more honestly and fully, just as David did?

2. **The Heart of Worship**

   One of the key lessons from David's life is that worship is not about perfection but about the posture of the heart. David was flawed, yet he always returned to God in worship, seeking Him in every situation.

   - Reflection: What areas of your life are you holding back from worship? Are there moments where pride, shame, or fear prevent you from fully surrendering in worship? How can David's life inspire you to offer every part of yourself to God?

3. **Worship as a Journey**

   Worship for David was not a one-time event but a lifelong journey that included moments of great joy as well as deep sorrow. He continually sought after God, regardless of his circumstances.

   - Reflection: How do you view worship in your own life? Is it an occasional activity, or is it a constant pursuit of God? How can you cultivate a mindset where worship becomes a lifestyle, not just something you do during church or spiritual highs?

Section 3: Journal Prompts

These prompts are designed to help you reflect personally on your worship journey. Spend some time journaling your thoughts and prayers as you process what God might be speaking to you through the life of David.

1. **Worship in Triumph**

   Write about a recent victory or moment of joy in your life. How did you express gratitude to God during that time? If you didn't, what could you have done differently to turn that moment into an act of worship? Ask God to help you celebrate His goodness more openly and freely.

2. **Worship in Lament**

   Reflect on a time when you were going through a difficult season. Did you bring your pain and sorrow before God in worship? If not, why? Journal your feelings about that experience, and pray for the strength to come before God with honesty and trust in times of hardship.

3. **Worship in Repentance**

   Consider an area of your life where you feel distant from God due to sin or failure. Take inspiration from Psalm 51 and write your own prayer of repentance. Ask God to create a pure heart within you and renew your spirit, knowing that repentance is also an act of worship.

4. **Worship in Loss**

   Think about a time when you experienced loss, disappointment, or unanswered prayer. How did you respond to God in that moment? Journal about how David's example of worshiping after the death of his child challenges or encourages you. Pray for the grace to worship God even when His plans are different from your own.

By engaging with these sections—digging deeper into Scripture, reflecting on the chapter material, and journaling your personal responses—you will gain a deeper understanding of how worship, in all its forms, can be woven into every season of your life, just as it was for David.

Chapter 8: Strength in Numbers: Worship in Community

1. Deeper in Scripture

Explore these passages to deepen your understanding of the concepts discussed in the chapter.

    1. Acts 2:42-47

        – Reflect on how the early church lived in unity, supported one another, and worshiped as a community.

        – Questions for study:

            What actions characterized the early church's devotion?

            How did their unity reflect their faith in Christ?

    2. John 17:20-23

        – Jesus prays for all believers to be unified.

        – Questions for study:

            How does unity among believers serve as a testimony to the world?

            What does this passage teach us about the importance of being "one" in Christ?

    3. Romans 12:4-5

        – Paul explains the church as one body with many parts.

        – Questions for study:

How does this metaphor of the body of Christ help us understand the role of unity in the church?

In what ways do our individual gifts contribute to the greater mission of the church?

4. Ephesians 4:1-6[BL 1-2]

   - Paul urges believers to live in a manner worthy of their calling, emphasizing unity.
   - Questions for study:

     What practical steps can you take to "maintain the unity of the Spirit" in your church community?

     How does humility, gentleness, and patience foster unity?

2. Reflection on the Chapter Material

Take time to process the themes and ideas from the chapter.

1. The Power of Corporate Worship

   - Reflect on your experiences in corporate worship. How does singing together in one accord affect your heart and spirit?
   - Think about how worship can transcend the walls of a church building. In what ways can you bring the spirit of worship into your daily life?

2. The Equation of Community

   - The chapter describes the church as unified + supportive = growth. Reflect on your church community:

     Is your church unified under Christ? What evidence of unity do you see?

How does your church support one another, both spiritually and practically?

In what ways have you seen growth, whether in numbers, spiritual maturity, or community impact?

3. Recalibrating Your Church

- Consider whether your church might need recalibration:

    Is your church truly founded on Christ, or has it become overly focused on routines and traditions?

    How can you contribute to fostering unity, cooperation, and inclusivity in your congregation?

3. Journal Prompt

Write your thoughts and prayers as you reflect on the themes of worship and community.

1. Personal Worship Experience

    - Describe a moment when you felt deeply connected to God in a corporate worship setting. What made this experience powerful?

    - How can you cultivate that same spirit of worship in your everyday life?

2. Your Role in the Church Community

    - Reflect on your role in your church. Are you contributing to its unity and growth, or are there ways you can improve?

    - What spiritual gifts or resources has God given you that you can use to support others in your community?

3. Recalibration for Unity

   - Think about areas where your church may need recalibration. Write down practical steps you can take to help foster unity and support within your congregation.

   - Pray for your church, asking God to reveal areas that need correction and to strengthen its foundation in Christ.

Chapter 9: Worship Through Song and Praise

Section 1: Deeper in Scripture

Take time to study the biblical passages that support the themes of this chapter. Use these verses to gain a richer understanding of worship through song and praise.

1. Ephesians 5:19

   - Read and meditate on this verse: "Speaking to one another with psalms, hymns, and songs from the Spirit. Sing and make music from your heart to the Lord."

   - Reflect: What does it mean to make music "from your heart to the Lord"? How can this become a regular part of your daily life?

2. Psalm 95:1-2

   - Study: "Come, let us sing for joy to the Lord; let us shout aloud to the Rock of our salvation. Let us come before him with thanksgiving and extol him with music and song."

   - Reflect: How does joyful singing express thanksgiving? How can you cultivate a heart of gratitude through music?

3. 2 Chronicles 20:21-22

   - Read the story of Jehoshaphat and his worship-led battle strategy.

- Reflect: How does singing praise invite God's power into our challenges? How can you apply this principle to your own battles?

4. Acts 16:25-34

- Study the account of Paul and Silas singing in prison.
- Reflect: What does their singing teach you about worship in difficult circumstances? How might praising God change your perspective during trials?

5. Psalm 150

- Read this psalm of praise that calls for worship with various instruments.
- Reflect: What does this passage teach you about the diversity and creativity of worship? How can you incorporate this into your own worship practices?

Section 2: Reflection on the Chapter Material

Reflect on the key themes and concepts from the chapter. Use the following questions to guide your thoughts:

1. The Gift of Music

- Music is described as a divine gift that allows us to connect with God. How has music shaped your own worship experience?
- In what ways does music allow you to express emotions or truths that words alone cannot?

2. The Biblical Foundations of Worship

- The chapter highlights examples of musical worship in both the Old and New Testaments. Which example resonates most with you, and why?

- How do these biblical accounts inspire you to approach worship through song in a new way?

3. The Power of Worship Through Song

   - The chapter describes singing as an act of love, spiritual warfare, and unity. Which of these aspects speaks most to your current season of life?
   - Have you experienced a time when worship through song brought you comfort, strength, or victory? Reflect on that moment and how it impacted your faith.

4. Living a Lifestyle of Praise

   - Worship through song is presented as a lifestyle rather than a single act. How can you integrate music into your daily walk with God?
   - What steps can you take to cultivate a heart that is constantly ready to sing praises to the Lord?

Section 3: Journal Prompt

Use the following prompts to journal your thoughts, prayers, and reflections.

1. Personal Worship Through Song

   Write about a specific worship song or hymn that has deeply impacted your faith journey. How has this song drawn you closer to God?

2. Music as a Tool for Gratitude

   Reflect on how music helps you express gratitude to God. Make a list of blessings in your life and choose a song to sing as a way of thanking Him for each one.

3. Worship in Trials

Think about a challenging time in your life. Did music play a role in helping you trust God through that difficulty? Write about how singing might help you face future challenges with faith.

4. Joining the Symphony of Praise

Picture yourself as part of the symphony of worship described in Psalm 150. How can you bring your "instrument" (your voice, talents, or heart) into this symphony?

5. Commitment to a Lifestyle of Worship

Write a prayer committing your life to worshiping God through song. Ask Him to help you make music from your heart, not just on Sundays but in every moment of your life.

Chapter 10: Worship and Sacrifice.

Study Guide: Worship and Sacrifice

Section 1: Deeper in Scripture

Explore these passages to deepen your understanding of sacrificial worship and its significance in both the Bible and your daily life.

1. Hebrews 13:15

   - *Key Question:* What does it mean to offer a "sacrifice of praise"? How can you apply this in your current circumstances?

   - *Challenge:* Memorize this verse and reflect on how it shapes your view of worship.

2. Mark 12:41–44 (The Widow's Offering)

   - *Key Question:* Why did Jesus commend the widow's offering? How does her example challenge your perspective on giving and worship?

- *Challenge:* Identify one way you can give sacrificially—of your time, talents, or resources—this week.

3. Job 1:20-21 (Job's Worship in Loss)
    - *Key Question:* How does Job's response to loss demonstrate the essence of sacrificial worship?
    - *Challenge:* Reflect on a time when you faced loss or hardship. How did your response compare to Job's?

4. Acts 16:25-34 (Paul and Silas in Prison)
    - *Key Question:* How did worship transform Paul and Silas's dire situation? What does this teach about the power of praise in trials?
    - *Challenge:* Choose a worship song that resonates with your heart during tough times. Sing or meditate on it this week as an act of praise.

Section 2: Reflection on the Chapter Material

Use these questions to connect the chapter's themes with your own experiences.

1. Recognizing Sacrifices in Daily Worship
    - How do your daily choices reflect worship?
    - Consider the example of guiding a loved one through a major life decision (like Landry joining the Air Force). Have you experienced a similar moment? How did your faith shape your response?

2. The Cost of Praise
    - Reflect on a time when praising God felt difficult. What emotions or circumstances made it a sacrifice?

  - How did worship in that moment impact your perspective or strengthen your faith?

3. Practicing Gratitude in Trials

  - Recall a challenging season in your life. What blessings did you find during that time?

  - How does focusing on gratitude shift your mindset in the face of uncertainty or hardship?

4. The Widow's Offering in Action

  - Have you ever witnessed or participated in sacrificial giving like the military families who supported others during deployment?

  - What does this kind of generosity teach about trusting God with our resources?

Section 3: Journal Prompts

Take time to reflect and write about these prompts. Let them guide you deeper into worship and sacrificial living.

1. The Heart of Worship

  - Write about a moment when you felt closest to God during a difficult season. What role did worship play in that experience?

2. Gratitude in Trials

  - List three things you're thankful for today, even if life feels heavy. How does this list reflect God's faithfulness in your life?

3. Your Sacrifice of Praise

   - What is one area of your life where you feel God is calling you to bring a "sacrifice of praise"? Describe what that might look like and how you can take the first step.

4. Generosity in Worship

   - Reflect on a time when you gave sacrificially—of your time, energy, or resources. How did that act of worship impact you or others?

   - Write about one way you can give sacrificially this week, trusting God to provide.

5. Surrender and Trust

   - Are there fears or uncertainties in your life that you need to surrender to God? Write a prayer of trust, giving those concerns to Him and praising Him for His faithfulness.

Chapter 11: Worship as Intersession

Section 1: Deeper in Scripture

Use these passages to explore the biblical foundation of intercessory worship. Reflect on how each text expands your understanding of worship as an act of intercession.

1. Isaiah 56:7

   - *Key Verse:* "For my house will be called a house of prayer for all nations."

   - Reflection Question: How does this verse reveal God's vision for worship as a global and inclusive act? What does it mean for you to participate in this kind of worship?

2. Genesis 18:22–33

   – *Abraham Interceding for Sodom*: Explore how Abraham's dialogue with God reflects reverence, boldness, and a deep sense of justice.

   – Reflection Question: How can you emulate Abraham's heart for others in your own prayers during worship?

3. Exodus 32:11–14

   – *Moses Pleads for Israel*: Consider Moses' intercession for Israel after their sin with the golden calf.

   – Reflection Question: What does Moses' example teach about standing in the gap for others, even when they are undeserving?

4. Acts 12:5–17

   – *The Church Prays for Peter*: Study how the early church united in prayer for Peter's deliverance.

   – Reflection Question: What role does collective prayer play in your church's worship? How can your community grow in intercessory worship?

5. Psalm 22:3

   – *God Inhabits Praise*: Reflect on how praise creates a dwelling place for God's presence.

   – Reflection Question: How does your worship invite God's presence into specific situations?

Section 2: Reflection on the Chapter Material

Reflect on these themes from the chapter and consider how they apply to your life.

1. Worship as Advocacy

   Worship moves beyond personal devotion when it becomes a bridge between heaven and earth for others. Think about a time when worship helped you intercede for someone else.

   - Reflection Question: How has God used your worship to impact others?

2. Sensitivity to the Spirit

   The Holy Spirit often guides us to specific needs during worship. Reflect on moments when you've felt the Spirit prompting you to pray for someone or something.

   - Reflection Question: How can you cultivate greater sensitivity to the Spirit's leading during worship?

3. Corporate Worship's Power

   Worshipping with others amplifies intercession and aligns hearts with God's purposes. Consider how your church engages in intercessory worship.

   - Reflection Question: What steps can your church take to become a "house of prayer for all nations"?

4. Creative Worship

   Intercessory worship can take many forms, including art, poetry, and song. Reflect on how creativity can enhance your worship and intercession.

   - Reflection Question: What creative expressions of worship could you explore to deepen your intercession?

5. Personal Growth Through Intercession

   Intercessory worship transforms the worshiper, aligning their heart with God's compassion and purposes.

   - Reflection Question: How has intercessory worship changed your perspective on prayer and praise?

Section 3: Journal Prompts

Use these prompts to write and reflect on your journey with intercessory worship.

1. **Your Role as an Intercessor**

   Reflect on Isaiah 56:7 and God's vision for His house as a house of prayer for all nations.

   - Prompt: Write about how you see your role as an intercessor in worship. What steps can you take to align with God's mission?

2. **A Time of Intercession**

   Think about a specific moment when you felt called to intercede for someone during worship.

   - Prompt: Describe the experience. How did it impact you and the person or situation you prayed for?

3. **Listening to the Spirit**

   Consider how the Holy Spirit has guided you in intercession during worship.

   - Prompt: Write about a time when the Spirit led you to pray for someone or something unexpectedly. How did you respond?

4. **Corporate Worship Reflection**

   Reflect on your experience in corporate worship and its power to unite believers in intercession.

   - Prompt: How has worship with others encouraged or strengthened your prayers for others?

5. **Creative Acts of Intercession**

   Explore how you can use creativity in intercessory worship.

- Prompt: Write about a creative act of worship you could offer as intercession for someone or something. How would it express your heart and faith?

6. Personal Transformation Through Worship

   Intercessory worship not only impacts others but also transforms the worshiper.

   - Prompt: How has intercessory worship shaped your faith, character, or understanding of God's heart?

Closing Encouragement

Let these exercises deepen your understanding and practice of intercessory worship. Through Scripture, reflection, and journaling, embrace your role as a worshiper who stands in the gap for others, lifting their needs to the throne of grace. Worship with boldness, creativity, and compassion, trusting that God hears and moves through your prayers and praise.

Chapter 12: The Eternal Worship of Heaven

Section 1: Deeper in Scripture

Use these questions and prompts to explore the biblical foundations of this chapter more thoroughly. Take time to read and meditate on the referenced passages.

1. Read Revelation 4:1-11.

   - What stands out to you about John's description of the throne room?

   - How does the imagery of the throne, the creatures, and the elders expand your understanding of God's sovereignty and holiness?

2. Explore the meaning of God's holiness.

   - Look up Isaiah 6:1-4 and compare it to Revelation 4:8. How does the repeated cry of "Holy, holy, holy" emphasize the uniqueness of God?

   - Read Exodus 15:11. How does this passage reinforce the idea of God's holiness and majesty?

3. Consider the symbolism of the elders casting their crowns.

   - Read 1 Corinthians 9:25 and James 1:12, which mention crowns. What do these crowns represent, and why is it significant that the elders lay them before God?

   - How does this act of surrender shape your understanding of worship as giving back to God what He has given us?

4. Reflect on unceasing praise.

   - Read Psalm 145:1-7. How does David's declaration of God's greatness mirror the unceasing worship in Revelation 4?

   - What practical ways can you incorporate the principle of "unceasing praise" into your daily life?

Section 2: Reflection on the Chapter Material

Use these questions to engage with the themes and lessons discussed in the chapter. Reflect on how these truths apply to your life.

1. John's earthly circumstances versus heavenly vision.

   - How does John's exile on Patmos shape your perspective on the way God can reveal Himself in times of difficulty?

   - Have you ever experienced a moment where God's presence felt especially close despite challenging circumstances? How did that experience transform your outlook?

2. The centrality of the throne.

    - The throne in Revelation 4 represents God's sovereignty and authority. In your own life, what competes with God for the "throne" of your heart?

    - How can recognizing God's sovereignty help you trust Him more fully in uncertain times?

3. Reverence and awe in worship.

    - In what ways has your approach to worship been casual or routine? How does the heavenly worship described in Revelation challenge you to approach God with greater reverence?

    - Think about a time when you were in awe of God's greatness. What triggered that sense of awe, and how did it affect your worship?

4. Casting crowns in surrender.

    - The elders cast their crowns before God's throne as an act of surrender and acknowledgment of His worthiness. What "crowns" in your life—achievements, ambitions, or possessions—might you need to surrender to God?

    - How can surrendering these things bring you closer to experiencing true worship?

5. Living a life of unceasing praise.

    - The creatures in Revelation worship God day and night. While constant singing may not be possible, how can your everyday actions and attitudes reflect continual worship?

    - What changes might you need to make in your daily routine to cultivate a mindset of worship?

Section 3: Journal Prompt

Use these prompts to guide personal journaling and deepen your spiritual growth based on this chapter.

1. Write about a time when you felt particularly connected to God during worship. What made that moment stand out, and how did it reflect the themes of reverence and awe?

2. Reflect on the idea of God's throne as the center of all creation. If your life were organized around God's throne, what changes would you need to make in your priorities, relationships, and habits?

3. Spend time journaling about the "crowns" in your life. What are the things you take pride in or hold onto for significance? How can you symbolically cast these crowns at God's feet in surrender?

4. Imagine yourself in the heavenly scene described in Revelation 4. Picture the throne, the living creatures, and the elders casting their crowns. Write a prayer or poem inspired by this vision, expressing your gratitude and reverence for God.

5. Create a plan for how you can incorporate the principle of unceasing worship into your daily life. This might include specific practices like morning prayers of adoration, gratitude journaling, or choosing worshipful music during your commute. Write down your plan and commit to it for the next month.